TWAYNE'S WORLD AUTHORS SERIES

A Survey of the World's Literature

Sylvia E. Bowman, Indiana University

GENERAL EDITOR

FRANCE

Maxwell A. Smith, Guerry Professor of French, Emeritus
The University of Chattanooga
Former Visiting Professor in Modern Languages
The Florida State University

EDITOR

Arthur Adamov

TWAS 318

Arthur Adamov

Arthur Adamov

By JOHN H. REILLY

Queens College of the City University of New York

Twayne Publishers, Inc.　:　:　New York

Library of Congress Cataloguing in Publication Data

Reilly, John H.
  Arthur Adamov

  (Twayne's world authors series, TWAS 318)
  Bibliography: p.170.
  1. Adamov, Arthur—Criticism and interpretation.
PQ2601.D323Z88   842'.9'14   74–2162
ISBN 0-8057-2005-7

Contents

About the Author

John H. Reilly received his B.A. degree from Syracuse University and the M.A. and Ph.D. degrees from the University of Wisconsin. He has taught at the latter institution and at Bowling Green State University, and is presently Associate Professor of Romance Languages at Queens College of the City University of New York. Professor Reilly has prepared a text edition of Jean Giraudoux's *Intermezzo* and has also published articles in the *French Review*. In addition, he is the American contributor to the bibliography of the *Revue d'Histoire du Théâtre*. His fields of interest include the contemporary French theater as well as contemporary European and American theater.

* * *

To My Parents

Preface

During the 1950's, the French theater was bursting with energy and vitality. The new playwrights of the avant-garde were turning the stage into an imaginative and inventive arena for the discussion of the human condition. Three of the major dramatists of the period were the Irish-born Samuel Beckett, the Roumanian-born Eugène Ionesco and the Russian-born Arthur Adamov. In the following years, both Beckett and Ionesco went on to become permanent figures in the theater of the absurd and countless books and articles have appeared on them all over the world. During this same time, however, Adamov's work generated very few articles and, as of this writing, only two book-length studies in French. While it is now clear that Adamov does not rank with Beckett and Ionesco as was originally thought, it is nevertheless evident that he is a substantial figure in the history of the French theater and that his work deserves consideration.

Indeed, it would be an injustice to ignore the feverish, intense creativity which the Russian playwright brought to the French stage. A man of enormously paralyzing neuroses, he used literature as a form of catharsis, a means of purging his soul from the anguish and torment which life had brought him. Adamov was a person who had a tremendous desire for life, but who found it difficult to make contact with people and objects around him. Yet, paradoxically, his work is oftentimes stunning in its honest and direct communication of the torture of living.

Rarely has the theater been used so forcefully as the anguished cry of human existence. While Adamov's work is frequently unsuccessful in its final effect, it is nonetheless true that his writing is very bold, innovative, and exciting. A man of many models and masters (August Strindberg, Antonin Artaud, Bertolt Brecht, Karl Marx among others), he merged them all with his own unique personality to create a decidedly individualistic expression; each one of his plays was an almost rebellious attempt to re-create and reshape the form of theater in light of his own view of the world. No two of his works are alike, not only because of the many facets of the dramatist's personality, but because Adamov was constantly experimenting with the technical possibilities of the stage. His plays are never boring— confusing, exasperating, frustrating at times, but always alive with a pain-filled emotion.

Adamov was a mercurial, enigmatic figure given to strong, exaggerated opinions. Further, he was in the most unusual position of having totally repudiated his first few plays. Having turned to the theater as a means of coping with his neuroses, his first works were very personal, introspective, and self-oriented. The playwright then redirected his goals and wrote dramas which were politically committed, containing a strongly Marxist overtone. At this point, he announced that he rejected his early writings because they took place in a "no-man's-land" and had little or no contact with reality. Shortly after this, he revised his position once again and combined both the personal and the political in his theater.

This study follows the author's development and the discussion of Adamov's theater is consequently divided into the three "phases" of his writing. It is understood, however, that any such divisions are somewhat arbitrary and are utilized merely as useful guidelines or reference points in presenting the writer's essentially unified dramatic output. Since the playwright's work is so closely connected to his personality, it always reflects the diversified and complex aspects of Adamov, the human being. As widely divergent as some of the topics seem to be, they lead back to the oneness of the author. Moreover, it is generally accepted by critics that these various phases of his plays were never very much separated, one from the other. Even in his early "personal" dramas, the political concerns were only slightly hidden beneath the surface. Later, the dramatist was able to sustain the strongly realistic tone of his plays for only two works before he was again caught in the web of his neuroses of which his political concerns were but one more manifestation.

In this study, I will present a literary analysis of all of the major writings of the author, centering principally on Adamov's theatrical efforts. At the same time, in the discussion of each play, I will deal with the interrelationship of the author and his works, for it is virtually impossible to appreciate Adamov, the writer, without an understanding of Adamov, the man. Most of the basis for this discussion comes from the dramatist's plays, his journals, and his own prefaces explaining the aims of his theater. This study is divided into six major sections: a biography, which presents the major facts of his life, especially as they pertain to his development as a writer; "the incurable evil," a discussion of the early works dealing with the neuroses and obsessions of the writer; "the curable evil," an analysis of the plays involving Adamov's economic, historical, and political concerns; "the synthesis," his final phase when he merged the personal and political; a brief conclusion, summing up and evaluating Adamov's position in French literature; and a selective bibliography, listing the first published editions of each of his works, as well as any important books or articles written about him. All the quotations from the writings will be in English and the translations are my own. Most of Adamov's plays have not been translated into English and the titles which I have provided are fairly literal translations. However, in cases where a literal translation might be misleading, a freer rendition was used. In all cases, the quotations from his plays and journals come from the most recent and most readily available Gallimard editions. Each of these editions is first identified in a note, and all subsequent citations from that edition are incorporated into the text of the study with the necessary reference furnished.

In presenting this analysis of Adamov and his works, I hope to indicate both the strengths and weaknesses of the writer. It is not my intention to place Adamov among the few major figures of Twentieth-Century French literature, for he does not belong there; he was too hermetic and too self-concerned to achieve a universal response among his audience or readers. But, Adamov dealt with the sorrows of existence, the pains of the human condition; and his writings are a sensitive expression of his own, unique personality. As such, he is a figure worthy of consideration, and it is now time to assess his contributions and to gauge his importance.

JOHN H. REILLY

Flushing, New York

Chronology

1908   August 23: Born in Kislovodsk.

1908–   Childhood spent in Baku.
1914

1914   Adamov family leaves for Germany. War breaks out and family leaves Germany for Switzerland.

1914–   Family lives in exile in Switzerland.
1922

1917   Russian Revolution.

1918   Nationalization of the oil wells of the Adamov family.

1922–   Family is forced to return to Germany because of lack of money.

1924   Adamov is enrolled at the French *lycée* in Mainz.

1924–   Family lives at Bourg-la-Reine, suburb of Paris. Adamov and
1927   school friend, Victor, publish article entitled "Vive l'anarchie" in journal, *L'En-dehors*. Adamov sends poetry to Paul Eluard and meets Surrealist writers. First short schoolboy play, *Mains blanches*. Meets Roger Gilbert-Lecomte, who becomes his good friend. Attends production of *The Dream Play* by August Strindberg, presented at Antonin Artaud's Théâtre de la Cruauté.

1928   Meets Irène, the first love.

1933   Writes poems for friend Meret Oppenheim, published by the *Cahiers du Sud*. Adamov's father commits suicide.

1935   Meets Marthe Robert.

1938–   First acquaintance with Franz Kafka's work. Translates Carl
1939   Jung's *The Relations Between the Ego and the Unconscious*. Begins writing his first major work, *L'Aveu*.

1940–   Flees German occupation of Paris. Goes to Marseilles. Arrested
1941   and sent to concentration camp in Argelès.

1941–   Liberated, returns to Paris.
1942

1942   Mother dies of tuberculosis in hospital at Brévannes.

1943   Death of Roger Gilbert-Lecomte.

1945–   Publishes a review, *L'Heure Nouvelle*, with Marthe Robert.
1946

1946   Publication of *L'Aveu*.

1947   Finishes writing his first major play, *La Parodie*. Meets Jacqueline Trehet, who will become his wife in 1961.

1948   Suicide of Antonin Artaud. Adapts Georg Büchner's *Danton's Death*, presented at the Second Festival in Avignon.

1950 Publishes *La Parodie* and *L'Invasion*. First presentation of plays on stage. November 11: *La Grande et La Petite Manœuvre* at the Théâtre des Noctambules in Paris under the direction of Jean-Marie Serreau. November 14: *L'Invasion* presented at the Studio des Champs-Elysées in Paris under the direction of Jean Vilar.

1951 Publishes *Le Désordre*.

1952 June 5: *La Parodie* presented at the Théâtre Lancry in Paris under the direction of Roger Blin.

1953 March 18: *Le Professeur Taranne* and *Le Sens de la marche* presented at the Théâtre de la Comédie in Lyon under the direction of Roger Planchon. April 14: *Tous contre tous* presented at the Théâtre de l'Oeuvre in Paris under the direction of Jean-Marie Serreau. Publishes *Théâtre I.*

1954 May: *Le Professeur Taranne* and *Comme nous avons été* presented at the Théâtre de l'Oeuvre in Paris under the direction of Jacques Mauclair. Writes *Les Retrouvailles*, never performed on stage. The Berliner Ensemble debuts in Paris, performing works by Bertolt Brecht. Beginning of the Algerian war.

1955 March 2: *Le Ping-Pong* presented at the Théâtre des Noctambules in Paris under the direction of Jacques Mauclair. Publishes study on August Strindberg. Publishes *Théâtre II.*

1957 May 24: *Paolo Paoli* presented at the Théâtre de la Comédie in Lyon under the direction of Roger Planchon.

1958 January 16: *Paolo Paoli* presented at the Théâtre du Vieux Colombier in Paris under the direction of Roger Planchon. Publishes three short one-act plays under the title *Théâtre de Société* (*Intimité, Je ne suis pas Français*, and *La Complainte du Ridicule*). Also publishes *Les Apolitiques*. Charles de Gaulle becomes ruler in France.

1959 Publishes *Anthologie de la Commune*. *Le Ping-Pong* performed in New York. Makes first visit to the United States in connection with production of his play.

1960 Publishes *Le Printemps 71*. Signs the *Manifeste des 121* against the war in Algeria.

1961 Marriage to Jacquie.

1962 *Le Printemps 71* performed in London.

1963 April 26: *Le Printemps 71* performed at Théâtre Gérard Philipe at Saint-Denis under the direction of Claude Martin. *La Politique des restes* presented in London under the title, *The Scavengers*.

1964 Second trip to the United States. Gives courses at Cornell University. Visits New York again. Publishes *Ici et Maintenant*.

1966 Is in bad physical shape. Frequent trips to hospital. Publishes *Théâtre III.*

1967 October: *La Politique des restes* presented at the Théâtre Gérard Philipe in Saint-Denis under the direction of José Valverde.

Chronology

1968   September 27: *M. le Modéré* presented at the Théâtre des Mathurins in Paris under the direction of André Steiger. Publishes *L'Homme et l'enfant* and *Théâtre IV*.

1969   January 25: *Off Limits* performed at the Théâtre de la Commune in Aubervilliers under the direction of Gabriel Garran. Publication of *Off Limits* and *Je ... Ils ....*

1970   March 15: Death of Adamov in Paris. Publication of final play, *Si l'été revenait*.

1972   May 17: *Si l'été revenait* presented at the Cartoucherie in Vincennes under the direction of Michel Berto.

CHAPTER 1

The Writer and His Life

I The Early Years

ARTHUR Adamov was born in Kislovodsk in the Northern Caucasus[1] on August 23, 1908. The son of a wealthy oil well owner of Armenian origin, Adamov spent his childhood up to the age of six in Baku, located on the edge of the Caspian Sea, and, until the Second World War, the chief petroleum center of the USSR. Besides his mother, father, and sister, Armik, the household was also made up of several servants and staff, and French was one of the languages spoken.[2]

Although he was born into a position of comfort and security, the future writer nevertheless found life fearful and threatening. The political atmosphere surrounding the Adamov family was terrifying: the Armenians were persecuted by the Kurds, a colony of people living in the region, and Adamov's father was also once wounded by members of an Armenian nationalist group which he refused to join. In spite of his family's wealth, Adamov was always afraid of being poor, a situation which he subsequently experienced for many years during his lifetime. He was afraid of growing up, frightened of the night, even fearful of his sister: "It was she who persuaded me that my room contained several zones, some of which were evil, and I was not to venture into them at any cost. I didn't dare go near the windows, approach the radiator, or look under my bed. If I broke these laws, I was lost."[3] Most important, the young boy developed a fear of sex which was to be the basis of many of his later neuroses.

His childhood insecurities remained with him throughout his adult life. The pattern of anguish was set in these early years, as he indicated in a story that he related of a time when he and his family were on vacation at a resort hotel in the Black Forest. One of the boarders, a young American girl of eighteen, took great pleasure in torturing a cat. A seventeen-year-old English girl, who was also staying at the hotel, took the cat in her arms and consoled it. The American then twisted the animal's ears while the English girl covered it with kisses, a game which lasted for hours on end. Adamov later commented that he identified with the cat, having already, at his then youthful age, felt the powerlessness and the impotence of the animal being tossed about in an uncontrollable situation.

At this point, when the family was in Germany, the First World War broke out. The King of Württemberg, who knew Adamov's father, intervened and the Adamovs escaped internment as enemy citizens, going to Switzerland, where they settled in Geneva.[4] Adamov spent the years 1914 through 1922 in this rustic country, which he thoroughly disliked. In this very important formative period, from the ages of six to fourteen, he continued to be plagued by self-doubt and extreme anxiety. Already a sensitive young child, he was acutely aware of being an outsider, a feeling which played such a central part in his later works. Basically, he remained very much within his own family circle and within the group formed by the Russian colony in Geneva. However, it was in Geneva and through the Russian community that the future playwright experienced his first contact with the theater. Georges and Ludmilla Pitoëff,[5] the famous director and his wife, were just beginning their theatrical career and had become friends with Adamov's parents. In later years, the playwright recalled particularly the effect of the Pitoëffs' production of *Macbeth*: "The actors hold real foliage in their hands. This is the forest which moves, this is also my first great remembrance of the theater" (*HE*, p. 21).

In 1918, the beginning of Adamov's forebodings of poverty came true when the Russian army nationalized all the oil wells in the Caucasus and his family was obliged to sell its jewels in order to survive. The family returned to Germany in 1922 in hopes of improving its difficult financial situation, but, as life became more and more precarious, Adamov's father turned more often to gambling, a weakness which had now become a destructive obsession. As his son reported: "I spend one out of every two nights looking for my father at the casino, my mother orders me to do it and I obey. But I really hated those casinos, and that stairway which went to the gambling room, and that pale doorman through whom you had to pass, and finally, my father, lying, cowardly and even more pale than the doorman: 'Go tell your mother I am winning and that I will come right home'" (*HE*, pp. 24–25).

Several important events occurred at this juncture which played an important role in the playwright's literary career. While at the

French *lycée* in Mainz, he met and became a close friend of Victor
A., who shared so many of his adolescent experiences and who was
to be the prototype for Victor in *Le Ping-Pong* and Viktor in *Si
l'été revenait*. Moreover, he was writing what was apparently his
first attempt at literature: a story of a boy of fourteen who, in order
to attract the attention of a sixteen-year-old girl, wounds himself
with some branches, and then rolls in the nettles. Even in this first
effort, Adamov associated love and masochism, eroticism and
suffering, all later to be merged with a sense of humiliation. In his
personal life, also, the young adolescent felt the need to harm
himself: "I purposely cut myself with a knife in front of the mirror.
A pleasure to see the blood come to the surface and flow out"
(*HE*, p. 26).

II   The Years of Experience

In 1924, the Adamov family moved for the last time, to Paris,
this somewhat peripatetic existence undoubtedly contributing to
the dramatist's own nomadic, transient life in later years. The
Adamovs finally settled at Bourg-la-Reine, a suburb of Paris, where
young Arthur went to the *Lycée Lakanal*, from which he was expelled
for cutting class too often. During this period, he and Victor
collaborated on an article entitled "Vive l'anarchie!" published in
the radical newspaper, *L'En-dehors*, and he began his strong lifelong commitment to political action by participating in a demonstration calling for the freedom of Sacco and Vanzetti. In 1927, he
became involved in the publication of a short-lived review called
Discontinuité, which also included Georges Neveux and Jacques
Prévert among its collaborators.

It was at this point that Adamov tried his hand at amateur
theater, partly because Victor had persuaded him that this was the
best way to meet girls. They rented the Studio des Ursulines where
his first play was performed: "*Mains blanches (White Hands)*,
which lasts five minutes. A girl, standing on a chair, takes the hand
of a boy, also standing on a chair. She lets it go, takes hold of it
again. This is already the theater of separation" (*HE*, p. 29).

Adamov's father would have preferred that his son become an
engineer, but the young boy's life already revolved around the
literary and artistic milieu. He spent much time in Montparnasse,
especially at the restaurant *Le Dôme*, where he met many talents of

the creative world, including the director Roger Blin, the sculptor Alberto Giacometti, and Antonin Artaud. [6]

Artaud—the playwright, the theoretician of the theater, the tortured soul—had a strong influence on Adamov's literary career in these early years. He was the first to introduce the future dramatist to *The Dream Play* of August Strindberg, presented at Artaud's Theater of Cruelty. In this work, with its dreamlike atmosphere and allegorical events, Adamov found inspiration for the form of his own future theater, recognizing the shape and the expression of his own nightmares on stage. Already plagued with the torture of a hostile world and the agony of existence, he discovered a new and overwhelming torment in his first physical contact with a woman: "She would like me to make love. I cannot do it, she weeps" (*HE*, p. 32). This bitter revelation of impotence found its first literary expression in *L'Aveu (The Confession)*, published in 1946: "It is impossible for me to penetrate the interior of the body of a woman." [7]

In spite of this, or perhaps because of this, the writer sought the companionship of women. In 1928, Arthur met Irène, his first love, with whom he lived for a few months. Even in this relationship at the age of twenty, Adamov was storing up experiences which would be an important part of his later works. Irène had a young German friend whom her mother wanted her to marry. When the friend presently came to Paris, and when he and Irène were leaving the theater, Adamov suddenly appeared and pretended that he was going to commit suicide, throwing himself under the wheels of a taxi, escaping just in the nick of time. This incident was not forgotten and was incorporated into several of his plays. Furthermore, it was Irène who gave Adamov his nickname "Ern" (Irène—Ern), which also reappeared in various forms in his later plays.

Although the writer was developing contacts with a world which opened up new areas for him as an artist, he was not able (nor was he ever able) to break out of the tight family circle which his mother, in great part, had imposed upon him. [8] This close link with the family was also to be one of the causes of the tremendously paralyzing obsessions which plagued him throughout his lifetime, obsessions which he tried to purge through his theater and his autobiographical works. One of the most traumatic events occurred in January, 1933, when Adamov's father poisoned himself, whether because of a gambling debt or out of despair over a future with little hope, Adamov was never sure. However, the son could not forget what had happened and bore tremendous guilt feelings. As late as 1967 he wrote: "I hated my father. Therefore, I killed him. For at least a year, I was sure of it. Even now, I'm not sure that it isn't so" (*HE*, p. 45).

Although his literary output was secondary to the great emotional and psychological crises which beset him during the next few years, he did publish in 1933 five short poems in prose, dedicated to Meret Oppenheim, a young painter and sculptor. In addition, in 1938, Adamov prepared a translation of Carl Jung's *The Relations between the Ego and the Unconscious*, while he began to take his first, more definitive steps toward his future career. At this time, he was living in the same hotel as his friend, Roger Gilbert-Lecomte, and later, much of the writing of this period was grouped together under the title of *L'Aveu (The Confession)* and dedicated to Gilbert-Lecomte. It is in the autobiographical *The Confession*, written between 1938 and 1943, that we begin to understand the anguish with which the playwright lived. This work, which Martin Esslin classifies as "among the most terrifying and ruthless documents of self-revelation in world literature,"[9] gives a brutally frank account of Adamov's neuroses, especially of his desire to be humiliated by women, his inability to have normal physical love, and, most particularly, his sense of suffering and separation. At this point, Adamov first became acquainted with the work of Franz Kafka and he was fascinated by one of Kafka's stories which was read to him by a friend. Certainly, Adamov could not have failed to react to the author of *The Trial* and *The Metamorphosis*, whose writings so closely represented many of Adamov's own feelings of guilt, anxiety, and isolation.

The years 1939–1941 were also influenced by the war and by Adamov's internment on May 8, 1941, in a concentration camp at Argelès for "comments hostile to the Vichy government." The prison camp for him was only an extension, an external representation, of his own inner torture. Literally removed from the rest of the world, he became aware that he was existing "separated from everything in a time when all is separated from everything else" (*L'Aveu*, p. 141). What especially amazed Adamov was that any one person could humiliate and torture a fellow human being, simply to simulate authority; such inhumanity overwhelmed and depressed the future playwright. In this respect, he was highly pessimistic about the human race, to the extent that he doubted that man could learn anything from his agony. The writer did not seem to take much interest in the specific reasons for the World War II conflict, but, rather, saw the war as an expression of man's continuing battle with a hostile universe. He was convinced that man's only dignity lay in his refusal to submit in body and soul to the laws of the cosmos. This may explain, in part, why he did not participate in the Resistance movement after his release from prison on Nov. 11, 1941. In addition, he had a pronounced distaste for the people of the Right who took part in the Resistance. After he learned of the existence of the crematoriums in Germany, he did feel ashamed and attempted to justify himself: "But, what could I do, be anti-German at the side of people like Mauriac, Aron, Saint-Exupéry?" (*HE*, p. 79).

Adamov's mother died of tuberculosis in 1942. In a pattern similar to the reaction to his father's death, he suffered enormous guilt feelings, perhaps even greater than before, because of his early close association with his mother and because, in the years preceding her death, he had not been in close touch with her. These feelings of guilt, mixed with a love-hate relationship, were to find their full expression in many of the plays. In recalling her death in *L'Homme et l'enfant (Man and Child)*, Adamov stated simply: "Death of my mother at the hospital in Brévannes. I will not see her anymore. Impossible" (*HE*, p. 75).[10]

Following the liberation of Paris, the writer became more and more involved in literary endeavors. He and a friend, Marthe Robert, published a review *L'Heure nouvelle (The New Hour)*, whose collaborators included Noël Roux, Jacques Prévert, René Char, Artaud, and Gilbert-Lecomte. *The Confession* was also finally published in 1946, marking his major commitment to literature. In 1947, Adamov's life took a turn for the better when he met his future wife, Jacqueline Trehet, to whom he dedicated most of his plays: "I gave Jacquie the nickname of 'Rhinoceros.' She didn't keep it for long, a few days scarcely. She kissed me [*Elle me 'bise'*], the word struck me. From then on, she had a new nickname: Bison. She has kept the latter name. Hope that she will keep it always" (*HE*, p. 88).

At this same time, Adamov began to write for the theater. The actual reasons for this decision have never been explained by the dramatist. However, it is known that he was reading Strindberg's *The Dream Play* and that, perhaps thanks to the Swedish writer, he was able to find theater in the daily scenes of the street: "What especially struck me was the procession of passersby, the solitude in the closeness, the frightening diversity of their conversations, of which I would please myself by hearing only odds and ends, which, when joined with other snatches of conversation, seemingly constituted a totality whose fragmentary characteristics guaranteed the symbolic truth."[11] Certainly, Adamov's friendship with Artaud must have played some role in his decision to write plays; he was also aware of the emergence of Jean-Paul Sartre and Albert Camus as playwrights. His friendship with directors like Roger Blin and Jean Vilar helped orient him in his new direction, and Vilar's production of Strindberg's *The Dance of Death* (1945) and Shakespeare's *Richard II* (1947) as well as Jean-Louis Barrault's presentation of *The Trial* (1947) by Kafka had a great deal to do with his choice.[12] Finally, the theater became a means to externalize even further the terrors which *The Confession* had first presented, with the result that Adamov probably viewed the stage as the next logical step in his effort to rid himself of his obsessions.

III *The Mature Years*

From 1947 until his death in 1970, he wrote twenty theatrical plays, several radio pieces, numerous translations and adaptations, a critical study on Strindberg, autobiographical and confessional works as well as a collection of articles on the theater. This heavy output reflects the author's strong commitment to literature during this period, at first as an expression of a psychic need and eventually as a means of stressing his political ideas.

Adamov's first play, *La Parodie (The Parody)*, 1947, was followed by *L'Invasion (The Invasion)*, written during the winter of 1948–1949. Jean Vilar, the director of the *Théâtre National Populaire*, was the first to become aware of the new dramatist's talent. Having read the two works, he praised Adamov for renouncing the "lace ornaments of dialogue and intrigue, for having given back to the drama its stark purity"[13] of clear and simple stage symbols. He contrasted this theater with Paul Claudel's and made the statement: "Let us ask the question then: Adamov or Claudel? I answer— Adamov."[14] Vilar encouraged the playwright to publish the two works with endorsements by authors of renown, and André Gide, René Char, Roger Blin, Jacques Prévert, and Jacques Lemarchand agreed to provide tributes. The strategy produced the desired effect of making the new author known to the reading public and Adamov's works were presented for the first time on the stage in rapid succession—Jean-Marie Serreau directed *La Grande et La Petite Manoeuvre* (*The Great and the Small Maneuver*) on Nov. 11, 1950, followed three days later by Vilar's direction of *The Invasion*. A series of plays followed, each expressing a dreamlike world of terror, persecution and nightmare, while recalling the absurdity of human existence: *Le Professeur Taranne* (*Professor Taranne*), *Le Sens de la marche* (*The Direction of the March*), *Tous contre tous* (*One Against Another*).

During this period, Adamov became involved with the literary and theatrical world. He met André Gide, who was particularly impressed with *The Invasion*, and he also made the acquaintance of Eugène Ionesco, another playwright who shared some of his concerns about life. Adamov commented that Ionesco had told him that he liked *The Parody* and Adamov returned the compliment by praising Ionesco's *The Chairs*. In spite of this promising beginning, their friendship lasted only two years.

In 1954, the first phase of Adamov's theater came to an end and he began to write plays with a decidedly political slant, a committed theater with a strongly leftist point of view, stressing the defects of the capitalist society. As was indicated earlier, the playwright had always been highly sympathetic to the positions of the Left and, in this respect, his political theater simply represented another aspect of his personality. For a time, his plays lost their dreamlike atmosphere and took on a strong sense of reality. *Le Ping-Pong* (1955) was the first work to provide a transition between the two periods of his writing and *Paolo Paoli* (1957) firmly committed him to this new direction. At this moment in his career, Adamov also met a new, young director who was to be closely associated with his work: Roger Planchon came from Lyon where he managed his own troupe, bringing to his craft great inventiveness and creativity.

Following the election of De Gaulle as President of France in 1959, the playwright took an even more pronounced position in support of the Left, attacking De Gaulle and his group as Fascists. His theater of political commitment found its culmination in *Le Printemps 71* (*Spring 71*), an extraordinary account of the last days of the Commune uprising in 1871, a play bearing the definite influence of Bertolt Brecht and his theater of alienation. Adamov's turn to the Left was not, however, strong enough to make him join the Communist party, as his wife Jacquie had done. He justified his refusal to become a member in this manner: "I also was planning to join the Party, but I hesitated. I was not really in agreement with it on some problems. And, then, my Communist friends told me that I would be of more use to the Party outside than if I belonged" (*HE*, p. 127). In truth, Adamov did not see the Communist party as the final solution to all problems and, like most artists, it is probable that he could not in any case adapt himself to the limits and restrictions of any political organization, Communist or otherwise.

As his plays grew more political (and, at the same time, more physically cumbersome and expensive to mount on stage), Adamov was performed infrequently. This was a source of great distress and only exacerbated the anguish which he normally experienced, as he commented in 1965 during a period when he was seriously ill: "I think again about my professional disappointment, a source in great part, I am sure, of my miseries. Just the same, it's much too unjust that someone has not revived *Ping-Pong, Paolo. . .*" (*HE*, p. 168). He did find some satisfaction in the fact that his plays received attention in both the East and the West: the United States, East Germany, England, Italy, Czechoslovakia, and Scotland all performed his works. In most cases, unfortunately, the results were not too successful, since the productions were not able to do justice to the complexities of the pieces. Most of the time, the playwright was forced to support himself through translations and adaptations. Some of these were strikingly effective and original: His first adaptation, *La Mort de Danton (Danton's Death)*, performed at the Second Avignon Theater Festival in 1948, was called by Jean Vilar one of the two masterpieces of adaptation that the *Théâtre National Populaire* had ever performed; *Les Ames mortes (Dead Souls)*, first presented by Planchon at Villeurbanne in 1960, based on the novel by Nikolai Gogol, was also a highly inventive and creative piece of writing in its own right. In general, Adamov utilized the Russian that he knew and translated works of writers like Dostoevski, Gogol, Gorki, and, especially, Chekhov, for whom he felt a special affinity. In addition, he also helped earn his living through his work for radio, including numerous adaptations and four original plays: *L'Agence universelle* (1953), written in collaboration with Jacqueline Trehet; *Le Temps vivant* (1963); *En Fiacre* (1963); *Finita la commedia* (1964).[15]

In 1963, his personal problems took a turn for the worse. While he still had the much-needed support of Jacqueline, whom he had married in 1961, he was unable to avoid many of the terrors which controlled him: "I am beginning to drink heavily this time. I keep losing my memory, I no longer know where I live. Every night, friends have to drive me home" (*HE*, p. 149). His literary efforts continued, but took longer to produce: He needed three years to write *Sainte Europe (Holy Europe)*, which he finished in 1965. Nevertheless, in spite of his deteriorating physical and mental conditions, he continued to refine and develop his theater. From 1962 on, Adamov had started a new phase of writing. It was during this time that the playwright sought to achieve a balance in his theater between the political, to which he was firmly attached, and the personal obsessions, from which he could not escape. Making a conscious effort to merge the two phases of his writing into the single entity which they really were, Adamov wrote *La Politique des restes (The Politics of Waste)*, *M. le Modéré (The Moderate)*, *Sainte Europe (Holy Europe)*, *Off Limits*, and his final work, *Si l'été revenait (If Summer Should Return)*, a fairly impressive list in spite of his illness.

Adamov moved into an apartment in 1967 for the first time in his adult life. Up to that point, he had lived in hotels and had led a somewhat peripatetic existence with frequent trips to the south of France, two visits to the United States ("New York frightens me"), a voyage to Cuba ("Socialism under the sun. The gaiety of the first days of the Commune of Paris are found again"), Italy, and Scotland. Now, he settled down in his apartment and wrote the first part of *Man and Child*. The second part was a journal which he kept from 1965 to 1967, during the time that he was in the hospital. Even near the end of his life, he was writing a play on Ferdinand de Lesseps and was continuing his journal.

On March 15, 1970, Arthur Adamov died, a result of an excessive dose of barbiturates.[16]

CHAPTER 2

The Incurable Evil

WHEN Adamov first turned to literature, it was in the hopes of expressing what he saw as the *mal incurable* (incurable evil) of living: Man is placed in a world over which he has no control, he must follow an existence that he cannot really guide. Time, the inexorable enemy, fights him at every turn and destroys any opportunity to understand. Man is ineluctably led to his final destiny, death, a prisoner and a stranger. In this first phase of his writing, closely linked to his neuroses and obsessions, oftentimes sexual, Adamov saw the human being as an object manipulated by hostile forces—forces from outside (fate) and from within (psychic and emotional disorders). In either case, the true nature of man's tragedy is that he can do nothing about their power over him. Helpless, impotent, he is in total anguish, unable to cope. It was in this state of mind that Adamov composed his first few works, which bear testimony to the writer's dark, despairing, overwhelmingly sad view of life, an attitude which was to remain with him throughout his literary career, albeit ultimately, in a more moderate and controlled form.

I *Man's Desolation:* L'Aveu (The Confession)

Adamov's first major contribution to literature, *L'Aveu* (*The Confession*), written between 1938 and 1943, is composed of four sections: "Ce qu'il y a" (What There Is), 1938; "L'Humiliation sans fin" (Endless Humiliation), 1939; "Le Temps de l'ignominie" (Time of Ignominy), 1939–1940; "Journal terrible" (Frightful Journal), 1939–1943. Part of the latter section was written following his internment in the prison camp of Argelès.

This brutal and ruthless self-confession was an initial means for the author to liberate himself from his neuroses. The work, sometimes overpowering in its frank descriptions, reveals what the writer considered the major source of his illness: his awareness of a transgression which often took the form of a sexual guilt. This transgression, sexual or otherwise, was only a symbol of man's

25

greater and more tragic condition—that of separation, alienation, and exile in a hostile world. In order to combat the resultant feeling of terror and fear, Adamov had recourse to rituals, superstitious practices, and masochistic acts. Yet, eventually, he found that the only way to try to free himself was through writing. In describing his own obsessions, it was Adamov's hope that the expression of his sickness and torments would have a more universal application, that his work would be capable of defining more completely man's universal importance. As he stated in his Introduction, he would never have written *The Confession* if he were not sure that each person could find his own anguish expressed therein: "Neurosis being by nature an enlargement and exaggeration of a universal defect which exists in the embryonic state in every human being, but whose effects it multiplies and reinforces, my sickness, by its very nature, becomes exemplary" (*L'Aveu*, p. 19).

In 1943, Adamov commented that he had composed the work because he had wanted to express what had always been kept silent: He had intended to go beyond the normal limits so that man could know what these limits really were, to break with the primitive order, to violate original laws, in the hopes of finding a way to unify life's contradictions: "I wanted to write a book with no concern for boundaries which would limit such and such a particular subject, a book without limits in which I would express nothing but the essential, only that which emphasized my very reason for existing" (*L'Aveu*, p. 21). It would be his goal, he continued, to look at things in a new light, to find the basic matter when all else was stripped of illusory aspects.

The first section of the work, "Ce qu'il y a," begins with what Martin Esslin calls a "brilliant statement of the metaphysical anguish that forms the basis of Existentialist literature and of the Theatre of the Absurd":[1] "What is there? I know first of all that I am. But who am I? But what am I? All that I know about myself is that I suffer. And if I suffer, it is because at the origin of myself there is mutilation, separation./ I am separated. I cannot name that from which I am separated. But I am separated" (*L'Aveu*, p. 27). In a footnote, Adamov added that formerly the separation was from God, but now it had no name. Man is a stranger to himself, he has been betrayed in his integrity and must seek out the *alter*, the other, the one who is missing. However, time, with its inexorable flux, plays tricks, moving him from one superficial appearance to another and preventing any grasp of his own essence. There is within man this feeling of separation coupled with a violent sense of being torn apart. Adamov is aware that an invisible power is ravishing him— he cannot act, he is acted upon. Although he knows he exists, he does not feel any being within himself. Life seems like a "monstrous beast which penetrates and surpasses me, and which is everywhere, within and outside" (*L'Aveu*, p. 33). He does have one way, however, to rid himself of the terror which grips and envelops him: "My only recourse is to write, to make others aware of it, so as not to have to bear all of it alone, to get rid of a part of it, however small it may be" (*L'Aveu*, p. 33).

In his desperate attempt to unravel the awesome mysteries which life presents, Adamov sees the process of living as a series of contradictions, "movements of expansion, of withdrawal, of exultation, of depression, eternal rhythms of nature and of the heart" (*L'Aveu*, p. 34). The "movements of expansion" are reached through an understanding of the hidden meaning of space, which man attains by an intuitive awareness of his own internal space, particularly through the state of dreams, as Adamov notes in this Jungian-like statement: "The night dream is an open door on the great mysterious corridors of being and it is behind the door of sleep that the metamorphosis emerges" (*L'Aveu*, p. 43).[2] The dream becomes the means to help clarify life, to aid in the discovery of man and his position in the complicated process of living.

Besides dreams, the writer finds an awareness through his sense of "prayer," this "desperate need of man immersed in time to resort to the only principle that can save him, the projection outward from himself of that in him which partakes of eternity" (*L'Aveu*, p. 47). He must pray in order to find a being in himself who partakes of some eternal quality, which he defines as the point where all lives coexist with his. Pray, yes, but pray to whom: "The name of God should no longer come forth from the mouth of man. This word, damaged by usage for such a long time, no longer means anything. It is empty of all meaning, of all blood. . . . To use the word God is more than laziness, it is a refusal to think, a way of moving more quickly, a sort of hideous shorthand" (*L'Aveu*, p. 49). He is even reluctant to accept the word "prayer," but what else can replace it? Man, in quest of meaning, must empty his heart of all divine names, there being none for the obscure power which he implores. However difficult it may be, the only way to find value in life is through an attempt to grasp the few moments when one sees clearly, when one's perception has not been dulled. These moments of great lucidity are rare, and sometimes last only a second, continues the writer, in a statement which foreshadows Samuel Beckett's *Waiting for Godot*. As a result, one must try to prolong these moments so that their illumination can spill over into the daily routine of existence.

But the dreams and prayers are only one part of life's cycle— the moments of exultation are inevitably followed by the anguish of depression and especially by fear, particularly the fear of falling (*la chute*). In essence, Adamov concludes, man is afraid of anything which decreases or declines: silence, night, sickness, old age, and, finally, death. It is Adamov's contention that man is fearful of any movement which lowers him or implies a motion downward. And it is notably death which is the most frightening, for it is the time when man falls forever, for the last time: "This is the first and the only terror, the great horror of our origins" (*L'Aveu*, p. 36). For Adamov, the human being, the anguish of man is experienced in his almost morbid need to be humiliated by a woman he desires, in his willingness to throw himself at her feet, allowing himself to be stepped upon, if necessary, thereby undergoing physical distress while understanding, at the same time, the terrifying meaning of *la chute*. For Adamov, the writer, the decline of language is also a measure of our degradation, of our descent, since words have lost their original splendor and brilliance of meaning. However, words are still our last recourse and only they have the ability to say what is really meant. Nevertheless, they must be understood in their original meaning—and this will also be his task: to see an object until it loses its usual significance, until its appearances vanish. The essential is not to see things, but to see *through* them. His life may be a series of banal images, but it his responsibility to render these images eternal, to provide them with a lasting being.

In "L'Humiliation sans fin," the second part of *The Confession*, Adamov describes those facets of his life which are most closely connected with his neuroses, particularly the sexual aspects. In so doing, he attempts to exorcise the demonic spirits which possess him. By expressing his sickness, he hopes to free himself—not through indulgence or understanding, but rather, through total absolution. The author is convinced that at the root of the disease which controls him is "the awareness of a transgression and that this transgression is related to the mystery of sex" (*L'Aveu*, pp. 59–60). However, in the final analysis, this transgression is not his alone. It goes beyond "any individual feeling of guilt . . . surpasses the guilty person himself to identify itself with the transgression of all and forever: the great original breach of trust which has the name of separation" (*L'Aveu*, p. 60). Furthermore, in analyzing the French word for transgression (*la faute*), Adamov sees the word as meaning both "absence" and "fall," which he calls the two parts of separation, a definition which, in spite of his disclaimers, takes on a strongly religious overtone, reminding us of man's fall from grace in the Garden of Eden.

In this section, he proposes to defend the idea of neurosis, stressing its ability to provide a sharp lucidity, inaccessible to the ordinary man. Moreover, since the particular becomes a symbol of the universal, "the universal is most surely reached by the extreme of the particular, so that the neurosis which exaggerates man's particular vision defines more clearly his universal significance" (*L'Aveu*, p. 61). Having made this defense, Adamov then proceeds to discuss his neuroses in detail, especially those dealing with women. Basically masochistic, he is obsessed with the idea of suffering and humiliation, with the hope of falling to the depths; he wants to be in a demeaning and degrading position. To a large extent, woman helps him play this role. He sees her as the "other," whom he has been seeking, the stranger, the opposite of himself, the "eternal feminine" part of man which was amputated from him and which he seeks to reintegrate by possession of her body. At the same time, woman helps Adamov reach his goal of attaining the lowest depths, an aspect of masochism. She becomes the image of that which is sordid, possessing the attractiveness of an "abyss," very often taking on the form of a prostitute, whose milieu the writer often frequented. In this respect, he delights in being tortured and humiliated by the female: "For me, there is no voluptuousness greater than that of submitting, in its full force, to the indignity and scorn of a woman whom I hold in contempt, all the while remaining enslaved to the dizziness of the desire which she evokes in me" (*L'Aveu*, p. 74). Moreover, woman is able to humiliate him in a manner which he had not originally anticipated—he is not able to possess her physically: "To my inability to possess, she will answer by absence. I am condemned to solitude" (*L'Aveu*, p. 76). And this situation becomes merely the overt sign of man's relationship to the universe; man is already exiled, expelled by the mere fact that he exists. To exist means to be alienated; to exist is in itself a form of punishment. Referring to his parents' warning that if he touched his sex, it would be cut off, Adamov observes that castration is simply another form of the punishment which accompanies living: "To punish [*châtier*], to castrate [*châtrer*], a double aspect of a same original meaning. The fear of punishment can be reduced to castration. But, and this is the essential part, at the basis of any fear of punishment, there is death, the supreme castration" (*L'Aveu*, p. 75).

This need for humiliation and punishment is the result of Adamov's feeling of transgression and of the necessity for pardon, the combination of the two producing terror. Yet, he is not able to discover what transgression he must expiate. Thus the world becomes a hostile and frightening opponent: "The universe seems like an abstract scheme in which I try to unravel the lucky and unlucky signs" (*L'Aveu*, p. 81). This is why he must turn to a series of superstitious acts and gestures in order to hope to rid himself of the suffering (e.g., kissing the wood of his cane, touching the ground with the palm of his hand). Ironically, these gestures, meant to liberate him, leave him more bound than ever: "These useless gestures would be harmless if their constant care, the fear of forgetting them a single time, did not completely invade my consciousness, if they did not, little by little, gnaw away at the time in my life, casting out all freedom" (*L'Aveu*, pp. 87–88). In these superstitions, Adamov also sees a kind of struggle between light and darkness, which he traces back to an incident with his sister during their childhood. Just before going to sleep, he would say "Good night" to Armik. If she responded in turn, he had to repeat his "Good night." If she continued, so did he, since he had to be the last to say the words. Adamov remembers most particularly the fact that this by no means uncommon incident used to occur at night, the time of his greatest fear. He attaches tremendous importance to this struggle of light and darkness. First of all, as an adult, he cannot enter any closed room without having a lighted cigarette in his mouth, and "this is because there is a profound connection between the flame and virile power, since the humid and hollow obscurity which the flame fights symbolizes the somber mystery of woman's sex, the extinguisher of the flame. The survival of the light signifies the victorious swelling of man's sexual object penetrating the woman, and the particular importance that I attach to this ritual reflects only too clearly my fear of impotence" (*L'Aveu*, p. 91). But, he does not see this struggle of light and darkness as merely sexual, it is also a combat of human will. The lighted flame represents not only the desire for possession, but the will to greater being, the thrust for life beyond all obstacles. In its own way, the light becomes a means of avoiding the final darkness, death.

The third part of his work, "Le Temps de l'ignominie," written in 1939–1940, when the German invasion of France was imminent, attempts to define the period in which Adamov is living. In this section, the author tries to come to grips with his responsibility as a writer, which he sees as the necessity to call each item by its name, so that the real meaning, hidden until then, emerges. Further, he must "denounce . . . the degenerated concepts, the abstractions which are void of all life and have usurped . . . the dead remains of the old sacred names" (*L'Aveu*, p. 106). This will be difficult since Adamov views the modern period as one of degradation—in meaning, in language, and, most especially, in the sacred myths and rituals. These myths and rituals used to be expressed in religion, which transformed the most somber and bestial obsessions into a vital impetus: "Religions enslaved the obscure powers, preventing them from toppling thought into the abyss; they obliged them to play their role in the quest of the only goal: the march toward the greatest awareness" (*L'Aveu*, p. 111). While Adamov rejects organized religion or the idea of God *per se*, he nonetheless accepts the rituals and myths which provide a sense of past wisdom, a feeling of deep human truths, an ennoblement of man. The writer does see one hope in this hopeless period—perhaps everything that is now ignoble will be reborn in its ineffability, that which is now degradation may become exultation, repeating life's cycle: "Perhaps, the sad and senseless discourse that today's lifeless humanity spews forth will, in all its horror, in all its limitless absurdity, reecho in the heart of a solitary man who is aware, and then that man, suddenly realizing that he does not understand, will begin to understand" (*L'Aveu*, pp. 113–14). Faced with the horrors of the approaching war, man has nothing to expect from the external world; he must turn away from it if he wants to preserve his inner being from chaos. The only thing man can do is to strip away all the dead skin until he reaches his "great nakedness."

"Journal terrible," the fourth and final section, covers the period from 1939 to 1943, during the occupation of Paris, Adamov's incarceration in a prison camp, his release, and his return to occupied Paris. In this atmosphere, where hope seems so foreign, the author asserts that the only truth can be found in never waiting for anything and never hoping for any outside salvation. In this way consciousness escapes the power of time, this *mal incurable*, which is the basis of most anguish. For himself, he is aware that he must finish the pages which he is writing, he must express his own torture. Thus, "this testimony will bring to an unknown, to a man crushed like myself by the horror of living, the profound aid which other men gave me, men who, a short time ago, left, as I am doing today, testimony of their own torment" (*L'Aveu*, p. 121).

At this point in his life Adamov considers man's situation predestined, each person forced to follow a line which has been traced since his birth. It is impossible to want what is not destined, as it is even impossible to wish or want at all. The only thing one may do is to attempt to minimize the control over the individual. Pitiless time eats life away—what man has gained he can only lose; to attempt to retain something is the most useless of tasks. In this period of degradation, Adamov rediscovers that his suffering is augmented by another form of hell: absence. In the prison camp he finds himself separated from the rest of the world, and this literal, physical separation only reflects the real separation which everyone experiences. In a footnote, he adds: "These pages were drafted after my liberation from the camp at Argelès. At the camp, I would never have had the courage to write them; I didn't even have the idea of putting the slightest note on paper, nor did any idea of any sort come to mind, neither superstitious fears, nor desire for love, nor even the need for prayer" (*L'Aveu*, p. 141).

Upon his liberation from the camp, he finds that most of the people still remain in their own states of lethargy and indifference, even to the point of ignoring the horrors which surround them. This attitude is even more incomprehensible than the crimes which have been committed against humanity, and suggests to Adamov yet another task: "To penetrate deeply into the despair which characterizes this period" (*L'Aveu*, p. 148). The situation goes beyond that of the war—it reaches the very horror of existence itself. He recalls a moment on the subway when he looked at a man sitting opposite him. He could not help but think of the peculiarity of nature which created a man who was a complete stranger to him, and yet, in some ways, resembled him. Suddenly, Adamov had the feeling that the stranger was experiencing the same thoughts, regarding the same fathomless problem of the unknown: "This man next to another is alone, as I am alone. I think I understand that I am not alone in experiencing this, and thus my feeling is confirmed that fear is at the basis of all" (*L'Aveu*, p. 126). Indeed, this gives some measure of consolation. Man is like the leaves on the tree of which not one leaf is identical to the other and yet, they are all repeated endlessly. In this sense, the totality of mankind moving in the breeze of destiny obeys the same rhythm as the leaves of the forest: "These visions have the power to deliver me. They remind me of the presence of a universal harmony even as I am the victim of the worst discordances" (*L'Aveu*, p. 157). Yet such moments of consolation are brief and temporary. When writing this, at the age of thirty-three, Adamov saw his life as a reflection of emptiness: "What have I said or done which was worth being said or done?" (*L'Aveu*, p. 157). He has lived in anguish and estrangment. In this nothingness he finds only two justifications: the total love which he gives to a woman, and his desperate and ceaseless efforts to express his thoughts.[3]

Adamov later denied or rejected much of what he had written at this time. In 1968, following his decision to republish *The Confession* with some recent writings on the same subject under the title *Je . . . Ils . . . (I . . . They . . .)*, the author noted that he had always considered *The Confession* "a secret place in my work and, why not say it, a little like its water closet" (*L'Aveu*, p. 9). Although he felt that, over the years, he had been a little too harsh in his judgment, he still thought that there was a separation between the book and himself: separation in the sense that the work was too limited in its expression of his life, restricting itself to superstitious or sexual practices; separation because he tried to avoid reality; separation because he now (1968) rejected the metaphysical aspects of his confession, especially the rhetoric with which he enveloped his statements; finally, separation because he no longer could accept the idea of justification: "Justify myself about what? 'I am as I am,' said the song" (*L'Aveu*, p. 10). At the same time, the author saw some good aspects in his work: "In spite of all its faults, its grandiloquence, the crazy pride, the naïve pretention, yes, I do see a certain truth . . . . The succesful part of *The Confession* is when I display my childhood fears . . . . And also when I speak about the prostitutes . . . of the simple prostitutes who humiliated me in front of other whores or in front of men" (*L'Aveu*, pp. 11–12).

The Confession emerges as an incredibly honest and revealing work. In spite of Adamov's objections, it is the open and relatively straightforward expression of a man's personal feelings which most affects the modern reader. In this respect, this frank book is a thoroughly penetrating account of the difficulty of human existence and may be considered a major example of confessional literature. It is also a highly important statement of the basic anguish of the absurd and the sense of alienation in a hostile universe, preceding the theater of Beckett and Ionesco. Moreover, *The Confession* remains a remarkable illustration of the feelings of people faced with and living through World War II. While the writer concentrates on his own concerns, these feelings are easily representative of the inner torment of people confronted with the holocaust of the war.

In the final analysis, it may be that *The Confession* will remain as the most durable aspect of Adamov's efforts. Since all his writing is confessional in one manner or another, the semiautobiographical format of *The Confession* is perhaps the most suitable genre for the communication of his suffering. But, until he published *Man and Child* in 1968, this form was abandoned in favor of the theater, which Adamov hoped would provide him with a means of expressing more deeply and more imaginatively the sorrows of living.

II *The Theater of the Absurd*

In the late 1940's and early 1950's, when Adamov began writing his first plays, he was part of a lively and innovative eruption in the French theater. Several dramatists, while not forming a group, were nevertheless involved in creating a theater of the avant-garde, an anti-theater, or, to use Martin Esslin's term, a theater of the absurd. Eugène Ionesco's *La Cantatrice chauve*, Adamov's *L'Invasion* and *La Grande et La Petite Manoeuvre*, Michel de Ghelderode's *Sire Halewyn*, and Boris Vian's *L'Equarissage pour tous* began the deluge of new theater in 1950, followed by Georges Schehadé's *Monsieur Bob'le* and Ionesco's *La Leçon* in 1951, Adamov's *La Parodie* and Ionesco's *Les Chaises* in 1952, and Samuel Beckett's *En attendant Godot* (1953). This fertile and intense activity, supplied by playwrights as independent as they were creative, lasted throughout the entire decade. In no way did these writers constitute an organized movement in French theater, but they did find themselves in agreement on their outlook toward life as expressed in their drama. What all of these dramatists had in common was a feeling of metaphysical anguish, a sense of revolt, and a desire to revitalize the art of the theater, breaking away from accepted standards.

It is clear that there is no single definition for this new theater. Yet, a few major elements seem to be constant in most of the plays, and these same elements can be found in Adamov's own writing in this first stage of his career. Basically, this anti-theater wants to free itself from all forms of constraint in order to follow its own laws. In doing this, the playwrights reject the normal dramatic forms and feel free to eliminate the traditional concepts of characterization, language, action, and even time and place, if need be. The usual arrangement of exposition, development, peripety, and dénouement does not exist. Dénouement would be misplaced in any case since there can be no solution to problems which are, by their very nature, insoluble. More often than not, the characters in these dramas are stripped of any psychological traits, play no social roles, and are given only initials as names or provided simply with general titles to identify them. Language no longer fulfills its role of communication; it is now shown to be a means of non-communication—its emptiness and incoherence revealing the void and absurdity of existence. This theater of the avant-garde becomes a form of antirealism, presenting its own concept of reality through an irrational, tragic-comic presentation of life. In this imaginative world of absurdity, dreams and fantasies are created in ways other than through language itself. Most of the playwrights adopted Jean Cocteau's feeling for a "poetry of the theater" through nonverbal aspects, such as gestures, scenic movements, sound, lights, objects. This is a theater of distress, showing man unable to find the answers to his problems, adrift in a world both absurd and hostile.

The French stage has a rich heritage of innovation and revolt from the norm. Alfred Jarry's *Ubu-roi*, written in 1896, was probably the first and true precursor of the anti-theater. Written by a schoolboy mocking one of his teachers, the work is an attack on the cruelty of political and social authority, a reaction against realistic and psychological drama, and a foreshadowing of the plays of the 1950's. Jarry's comedy is willfully illogical, incoherent, and shocking;

characterization is absent, the characters cartoon-like, language inverted, and time and place distorted. This assault upon the bourgeois mentality in all its forms, including the theater, ranks as the first sign of total anarchy in modern French drama. Twenty-one years later, Guillaume Apollinaire's *Les Mamelles de Tirésias* (1917) continued the attack. In a sense, Apollinaire's play is even less logical and less rational than Jarry's. Apollinaire claimed that the work was a call for the repopulation of France following its decimation in World War I. In reality, the play was a revolt against the traditional forms of the stage, approaching the irrationality of Dadaism and Surrealism, the latter a term which Apollinaire supposedly coined to characterize this play. The dramatist accepted all of Jarry's innovations and went further. The work was to be a spectacle in which "Sounds gestures colors cries tumults/ Music dancing acrobatics poetry painting/ Choruses actions and multiple sets"[4] would be merged.

The third representative of this new spirit was Jean Cocteau who, rejecting realism, forged a theater of irreality and illusion, incorporating poetry, music, dance, and painting into his drama. In Cocteau's nonpsychological theater (cf. *La Machine infernale*), characters are dehumanized and all illusions are stripped away, forcing the spectator to abandon his usual attitudes toward theater and enter the dramatist's original and unique world.

The most creative and inventive personality of this early period was probably Antonin Artaud, whose work entitled *Le Théâtre et son double* remains one of the truly significant influences on modern drama. Artaud, through his contacts first with the Surrealists, especially Roger Vitrac, and then with the company of Charles Dullin, came into touch with a number of important figures in the theater who were to be profoundly affected by his sometimes exaggerated, but nonetheless compelling theories: Jean-Louis Barrault, Roger Blin, Jean Vilar, and especially Adamov. Artaud expressed many of the ideas which were to come to fruition in the theater of the absurd: rejection of a psychological and naturalistic drama; return to magic and myth to express certain hidden truths; creation of an awareness in the spectators of the chaos surrounding them, and reminding them that their lives are precarious; emphasis on the principle that theater must draw upon dance, song, and pantomime to evoke what is beyond the power of language; utilization of dialogue only as one means of depicting the inner mysteries, necessitating a new use of language in an unaccustomed fashion; importance of the *metteur-en-scène*, the director, who would be the supreme manipulator of all the elements. Artaud's Theater of Cruelty did not succeed during his lifetime, but one cannot read a play by Adamov, Ionesco, or Beckett and fail to see that his influence has been far-reaching and long-lasting.

Following the First World War, a great period of experimentation developed on the French stage. Four directors, called the *cartel des quatre*, dominated the time—Gaston Baty, Charles Dullin, Louis Jouvet, and Georges Pitoëff (Adamov's acquaintance from Geneva). Thanks to their innovative attempts, French drama became more experimental and less realistic, creating its own reality of poetry and dreams amidst the unreal. The outstanding playwright of this movement between the two world wars was Jean Giraudoux. In works like *Ondine* (1939), *Intermezzo* (1933), or *La Folle de Chaillot* (1945), Giraudoux succeeded in presenting his own fantasized view of reality, ignoring the normal theatrical traces of movement and character development. In this context, and in his own basically pessimistic view of mankind, Giraudoux would seem to be a predecessor of the theater of the avant-garde. However, he differed considerably from the playwrights of the new theater in his presentation of the human condition. Rather than the stark, grim portraits of mankind which characterized the works of the 1950's, Giraudoux camouflaged his despair via a brilliant use of elegant, witty language, and a stylized vision. And, although he made attempts to utilize the stage in a liberated fashion, he was not interested in creating an entirely new form of theater and was willing to use elements of the more traditional dramatic structure.

Giraudoux's theater of the 1930's could not express the horror that became evident in World War II. Faced with the events of Dachau and Hiroshima and a universe which might be blown to bits in a nuclear holocaust, the new dramatists could not allow their writing to remain indifferent to the harsh realities. With the start of the war, the playwrights at first turned to a more serious, more philosophically oriented drama in order to voice their feelings of despair and hopelessness. Both Jean-Paul Sartre and Albert Camus, writing shortly before and during the war, became the spokesmen for the philosophies of existentialism and the absurd, which were incorporated into the anti-theater. In plays such as Sartre's *Les Mouches* (1943) and *Huis clos* (1944), and Camus' *Le Malentendu*

(1944) and *Caligula* (1945), the two writers approached problems which were to be the concerns of the new generation: What is the situation of man in an irrational universe? What is reality? What is the meaning of the human condition? What is the definition of freedom? Like Giraudoux, both Sartre and Camus differed from their colleagues of the next decade in that they generally presented their ideas in a somewhat traditional framework in which dialogue and communication between people were central elements.

Not only were the events of World War II a grim reminder of man's inhumanity to man, but they very effectively reduced man's belief in a god, in a benevolent superior being; there was no longer a stability or solidity upon which to draw and to which to turn. As a result, the playwrights could not depend upon the established dramatic structure to express this new anguish. In a world in which man was aimless, even rootless, a different form of expression had to be developed—a form which presented the terror of being adrift in an alien world. To do so required a theater which was startlingly novel in its techniques and in its vision.

Adamov's decision to write for the theater at this period in dramatic history was sound. His sense of the suffering and the agony of existence in a senseless universe accurately reflected the attitudes of his time, and his introspective, bizarre vision with its anarchical, chaotic sense of structure coincided perfectly with the new aesthetic outlook.

III   *The Futility of Life:* La Parodie (The Parody)

Adamov began his first play, *La Parodie (The Parody)*, in 1945, completing the work in 1947. In this initial theatrical work, the dramatist admitted the influence of Strindberg: "At this period, I was reading a great deal of Strindberg—especially *The Dream Play*, a project whose ambition had seduced me" (*Th.*, II, 8). Later, in a study which he wrote on the Swedish writer, Adamov commented further on Strindberg's qualities which were very much like his own: "What basically does Strindberg want to do? He wants to affirm himself, to display himself, to prove, to escape. Where better to do this than in the theater?"[5]

It was a specific incident, however, which provided the author with the original inspiration for *The Parody*: "At the exit of the subway stop Maubert Mutualité, a blind man was begging. Two young working girls passed by, humming the well-known refrain: 'I closed my eyes, it was wonderful.' They didn't see the blind man and bumped into him. He tripped. I had the idea of the play that I wanted to write: *The Parody*. 'We are in a desert, no one hears anyone.'" (*HE*, p. 84).

This image of human solitude and lack of communication was to be the leitmotif of the play, both in the dialogue and in the visual presentation. However, once engaged in the writing, Adamov enlarged his scope and the piece became a deeper expression of his own personal torments. *The Parody* is an exposition of life's futility and absurdity, showing that all paths lead to inevitable destruction, whether the individual willingly accepts his fate or not. The work is a Kafkaesque-like demonstration of the terror of living, with man buffeted about in a hostile existence. In this respect, the play is the author's attempt to rid himself of his demons with particular attention paid to his personal desire to obtain revenge on woman in the figure of Lili. Finally, the work is also a form of rebellion against the so-called psychological theater, and an effort to create a new form, influenced especially by Strindberg and Artaud, with overtones of Kafka and the German Expressionists.

The composition of *The Parody* was not easy for the writer, and this first piece took almost three years, involving many revisions. While writing, he was never sure that he would be able to finish, as evidenced in his journal: "I cannot find the tone of the characters, it doesn't come. In despair, I sleep fully clothed, I no longer have even the courage to pull down the sheets" (*HE*, p. 84). Yet, eventually, he did achieve most of what he was seeking and, although not entirely satisfied, he noted that it was his first work, "it is thus rich, true." The play was to be presented in the spring of 1948 at the Théâtre de l'Oeuvre. However, the project was abandoned and the work was not performed until June 5, 1952, following the presentation of other plays by Adamov. When *The Parody* was finally presented on stage at the Théâtre Lancry, directed by Roger Blin, the production was a disappointment to the author and to the audience. Only Blin as The Employee succeeded in capturing what the playwright had hoped to see. Nevertheless, Adamov observed with some satisfaction in his journal: "*The Parody* gathered about fifteen spectators each evening; *The Chairs* of Ionesco, also performed at the Lancry, had about twelve" (*HE*, p. 104).

Rather than the customary plot development of the psychological theater, the playwright presents a series of expressions of feeling or states of mind, and not a sequential progression. As Geneviève Serreau states, "*The Parody* recalled certain *stationendrama* of the expressionist period where the succession of states of soul took the place of scenic action."[6] Nevertheless, there is a plot of sorts which does express the main themes of the play: the solitude and lack of communication and the futility of all endeavor. Arranged in twelve tableaux, the work recounts the parallel adventures of two men and their approaches to life, both ending in defeat and failure. The one, identified only by the initial, "N.," refuses to accept life and asks to be put to death as quickly as possible. The other, identified by his social function, The Employee, displays a simplistic acceptance of all that life has to offer and optimistically looks for the best in every circumstance. Both men gravitate toward the eternal female, Lili, who treats them with equal amounts of scorn and indifference. The action takes place in a large city with its concomitant feeling of anonymity and hostility, where time has lost any sense of reality (the city clock, one of the main objects in the play, has no hands). Two other characters, The Director and The Journalist, are also caught in Lili's spell and are treated with the same contempt. But whatever path is chosen, man's absurd uselessness is spelled out clearly: "N." is crushed by a car and his body is swept away by the sanitation department; The Employee ends up in prison, blind; The Journalist, disgusted with his life, is rejected by Lili and leaves, alone and abject; even Lili has become aimless and without direction. The Director alone seems moderately content at the end, possibly because he is the only one who has financial power.

Like Strindberg's *The Dream Play*, Adamov's work builds up, piece by piece, until it becomes a cohesive unity, held together by purpose and mood rather than by a developed plot. Like the Swedish dramatist, Adamov weaves a dreamlike pattern in which suffering and guilt are pictured as the leading aspects of the human condition with unrelieved sadness as the major corollary. In both writers' works, there is a strong sense of personal crisis and an important connection is established between the neurosis of the writer and the artistic expression of this neurosis.

Besides Strindberg, Antonin Artaud also probably had an influence upon the composition of *The Parody*. While Adamov does not reject dialogue as a basis for drama, like Artaud, he approaches it from a different perspective. It is seen as just one of the many aspects of the work and, at times, language is shown as a basis of noncommunication, as the characters respond at cross purposes with each other, never quite understanding what has taken place. The physical or visual action is emphasized as strongly as the verbal, and the dialogue is often utilized in counterpoint or juxtaposition to the visual.[7] Like Artaud, Adamov accepts all forms of stage activity and, while not attempting to encompass total theater in this, his first play, Adamov is clearly heading toward the idea of theater in multiple forms, breaking decisively with the "well-made" play.

To a great extent, Adamov's acceptance of Strindberg's and Artaud's vision of theater was simply an acceptance of those ideas which reflected his own complex, intricate approach to life. *The Parody* is an extension of the same personal problems which haunted him in *The Confession*: loneliness, suffering, futility, and a sense of impotence. None of the characters in the play has any communication with any other. Each one remains isolated in his own world and any attempt to break down this separation is futile. "N.," who presumably represents Adamov's own neuroses, cannot obtain anything from the others—he asks, but does not receive; he begs Lili to kill him, but cannot even communicate the idea properly. The universe appears a frustrating, inimical experience. Solitude becomes the one acceptable solution, as "N." comments: "But if, at least, they left me alone. What's the matter? What does this man want of me? What do they all want of me? And the other one, a little while ago, who confused me with his words? I didn't understand a single word he was saying" (*Th.*, I, 31–32). The Employee, on the other hand, even though he remains blissfully unaware, faces similar problems. He plans to meet Lili, although she has never agreed to an encounter. At one point, he thinks that the meeting is to be at the Royal Hotel, then the Continental Hotel, completely forgetting that she had accepted neither, entirely oblivious that no communication took place. Most often in the play, the characters speak *at* each other, but not *to* each other. Even though they appear to be addressing one another, their sentences do not mesh, their replies do not follow, the idea of the phrase is lost somewhere in the space between one statement and the other. One person will speak to a second, who does not answer, but a third will reply.

The resultant feeling of futility and absurdity is emphasized throughout the play. "N." is constantly portrayed as the abject sufferer, asking only to be relieved of his misery. His most recurrent position is prone, lying on the ground, inert, immobile. For him, there is no future, there is only yesterday, to which he turns in pessimism and despair, accepting all guilt. In sharp contrast (and a contrast which the audience is meant to be aware of visually), The Employee is movement, agitation, frenetic optimism, looking toward the better future, the happiness of tomorrow. Life for him holds the promise of renewed joy, a promise never fulfilled. In an obvious attempt at self-justification, Adamov, who portrays himself through the masochistic "N.," wants the spectator to understand that The Employee is equally as doomed to failure, that his optimistic approach is as futile as "N."'s pessimistic style. Even The Journalist, the one character who seems to have some sense of control over his activities, is defeated and remains as powerless as the others, Adamov once again projecting his own sense of helplessness.

None of the characters has any real direction over what happens to him, everything is in the hands of an absurd fatality, life is a parody. This parallelism for all, which Adamov later rejected as being untrue and untheatrical, means that no one can prevent the ineluctable total destruction which fate will bring. The one person who opposes this view, The Employee, is depicted right from the beginning as being unable to see properly, an overt symbolic indication of his shortsighted optimism and his eventual fate of blindness. Besides being a sign of man's inability to understand what is happening, this blindness, the original inspiration for the play, is also a reflection of man's incapacity to relate to his fellowman. The question of darkness and its contrast, light, plays a significant role in the work. In addition to the sightlessness which afflicts the Employee, the other characters are also fearful of this dark and are all seeking what René Gaudy calls the "light, the sun of summer."[8] But the season is autumn and darkness begins to envelop the play. In fact, the division between the twelve tableaux occurs at the moment of the arrival of night, when the characters can no longer see clearly, the night indicating the fatality which controls everyone. At the same time, when Adamov makes use of light, it is to present its harshness and to emphasize its power to clarify, to make people aware. The most striking example occurs at the end of the piece when the sanitation men sweep up the dead body of "N.," underscoring the final hopelessness of all men. In the stage directions, Adamov noted: "At the precise moment that the broom touches N., the light becomes very strong and very glaring" (*Th.*, I, 54).

Adamov found life a hostile and terrifying experience, and his first play expresses this feeling. The locale in which *The Parody* takes place, the city, offers unremitting animosity and instills fear in its inhabitants. The buildings look alike and the characters cannot find what they are seeking; police cars and sirens furnish unsettling background activity to the stage action; objects frighten the characters—clocks deny reality and refuse to provide time, The Employee tries to speak over the noise of a typewriter and his voice is drowned out, urban life becomes a jungle of movement. Even the spectators must be made to feel this dislocation. In his stage directions, Adamov specifically stated that the setting and production should create a feeling of estrangement, changing angle in every scene, in part to indicate that the audience is seeing the situation in different perspectives, but also to create a loss of identification, a constant impression of anomie. For example, the clock becomes larger as the play continues, taking on a more menacing and frightening appearance; the set itself becomes smaller until, finally, the acting area is found only in the middle of the stage, a powerful visual indication of man's loss of freedom.

Besides this expression of his basic fears, Adamov used *The Parody* to begin his literary attack on the role women played in his neuroses. In this play, Lili is the first of Adamov's female characters with whom there will never be any real human contact. In essence, if there is a structure to the play, it is found in Lili, the vortex, the axis around whom all the others revolve. In that capacity, she is man's quest, which can never be attained. The dramatist portrays woman as flighty, cold, mocking, unable to attach herself definitively to anyone, unwilling to give of herself. If Lili is to represent the justification of men's lives, then there is obviously none. If nothing can be created without her, as The Director and The Journalist indicate, then it is equally clear that nothing of substance will be created with her, since she is lacking in inner merit (a point which the dramatist would modify somewhat in later plays). Through the Prostitute, the only other female character in the play, Adamov provides an indication of how woman becomes part of his masochistic tendencies. "N." asks The Prostitute to walk over him, to smother him, to strangle him: "Last night, I dreamed of mud, of mud which was sick. It twisted with suffering. I am this mud . . . . Walk on me, kill me, so that everything will end" (*Th.*, I, 43). In the final part, "N." commits suicide by throwing himself under the wheels of a car, just as Adamov had tried to do over the love of Irène. Woman means humiliation for Adamov, she provides the degradation which he is seeking as part of his *chute*, the step before the final fall, death.

This first work by Adamov has never achieved any of the attention or success of some of his other works. It is too personal an expression of his problems and does not lend itself to a more universal theatrical experience. Since the theater was being used by the playwright as a form of therapy in an attempt to achieve emotional stability, the author was not able to overcome the fact that much of *The Parody* was significant only to himself. The bold effort to do away with plot and characterization actually helps to undermine the effectiveness of the presentation of the ideas, which were better expressed in the journal form utilized in *The Confession*. Nevertheless, this is a remarkably strong first play, particularly in view of the fact that the playwright did not depend upon preexisting established structures in the psychological theater, but set out to create a play along the lines of the theories of Strindberg and Artaud. Since such a framework is also true to Adamov's own vision of the world, the play, in spite of its complexity and frequent confusion, remains consistently authentic. The vivid visual use of the stage, while rendering the drama much less effective on the written page, nonetheless indicates Adamov's awareness of the potential of theater and suggests future promise.

IV *Deciphering the Indecipherable:* L'Invasion (The Invasion)

This promise quickly became a reality with his second play, *L'Invasion* (The Invasion), written in 1948–1949 and published along with *The Parody* in 1950. It was Jean Vilar who recommended to the young author that he use the publication of the two works as a means of making a reputation for himself. The strategy worked and Adamov's name began to be known in literary circles. Through the patronage of wealthy benefactors, two of his plays were presented at the same time in Paris: directed by Vilar, *The Invasion* was performed at the Studio des Champs-Elysées on November 14, 1950, three days after the presentation of *La Grande et La Petite Manoeuvre*, his third work. Beginning at 6:30 P.M. (since it was less expensive to rent the theater at that time), *The Invasion* was hardly produced under the best of circumstances. Adamov himself had lost interest and rarely attended the rehearsals, preferring instead to follow the progress of *The Great and the Small Maneuver*. When *The Invasion* appeared on stage, the playwright called it a fiasco, an opinion which reflected his own disenchantment with the work rather than a considered judgment of the production. He did mention, however, that the direction of Vilar gave him the "painful impression of seeing actors moving vaguely at what seemed like a distance of many kilometers" (*HE*, p. 98).

With his second play, Adamov made a decided attempt to create characters who were more human and less schematic. As he pointed out, "After *The Parody*, thinking that I had resolved the whole destiny of humanity with a single stroke, and still wanting to write for the theater, I decided to take a particular subject as the basis of *The Invasion*" (*Th.*, II, 9). The inspiration for the play may have come from a number of sources. The basic subject, that of a man trying to decipher the manuscript of a friend who has died, could very well have come from the death of Adamov's close acquaintance, Roger Gilbert-Lecomte. According to Roger Blin, Adamov had tried to gather together Gilbert-Lecomte's papers after his death, but had found the task perplexing and, eventually, impossible.[9] It is also significant that Adamov was writing this play at the time of the death of Antonin Artaud and this, too, may have provided some of the inspiration. Or, as Geneviève Serreau suggests, Adamov may have thought of the case of Max Brod, who took charge of the writings of Kafka after he had died.[10]

In this second work, the playwright is still pursuing the themes of *The Parody*, stressing again the lack of communication between people in this alien world, pointing out that the quest for meaning in life is hopeless and that any search for a sense of direction is a waste of time. Just as *The Parody* shows that all paths lead to failure, *The Invasion* takes a variation on the theme, demonstrating that any specific effort by man to understand his existence ends up as an absurd act. This second play, richer and more human than the first work, is, as a result, more accessible also. Whereas *The Parody* is an abstract, almost lifeless presentation of an idea, *The Invasion* is a more direct, more immediate expression of the playwright's feelings. In an obvious self-criticism, Adamov emphasizes the destructiveness of man's obsessions, which take hold of his life and make him useless. And the author individualizes the play more by limiting his subject to the family circle and underlining the plight of the writer who is rendered creatively and psychologically impotent by the "invasion" into his life of relatives and friends. Within this family grouping, the woman reappears in the roles of the wife and mother, who becomes an important figure for the first time.

In *The Invasion*, Adamov follows a more traditional dramatic technique. The plot has a sense of progression and the characters are more substantial, although the dramatist makes no attempt to give them the solidity which they might possess in psychologically-motivated drama. The action centers around the members of a family and the disruption in their lives caused by the manuscript of a writer, Jean, who has recently died. Jean has left his papers to Pierre, the husband of his sister, Agnès. It is Pierre's responsibility to decipher the manuscript, but the task proves impossible: much of the writing is illegible or has simply faded with the passage of time. In addition, Tradel, Pierre's friend, who is also working on the project, does not mind inventing whatever he cannot understand, leaving the real interpretation more hopelessly jumbled than ever. While Pierre is entangled in this insurmountable project, his personal life has become a nightmare because of the never-ending "invasion" by others. His household is a series of disorders, seemingly caused by his wife who is in constant conflict with his mother. In the midst of all this, a man appears, looking for someone in the apartment next door. This man, identified only as "the first one who comes along," stays in the room, invading Pierre's privacy even more. In an attempt to work in quiet, Pierre retreats first to a café, then to a room in the back of the house. At this point, Agnès leaves her husband, setting out with "the first one who comes along." With the departure, order has been reestablished and the mother has become the dominant figure. However, Pierre has now decided to abandon his work. In an effort to show the complete futility of all that he has been doing, he tears up the manuscript, returning to his room, once again withdrawing from society. As he does so, Agnès reappears, asking to borrow his typewriter, mentioning that her life with her lover has not worked out well, for he has fallen sick and she cannot manage his business. The mother refuses to allow Agnès to take the typewriter and she leaves. Tradel, in search of Pierre, finds him dead in his room, a suicide.

Like Lili, who acted as the axis in *The Parody*, the dead writer's manuscript remains the center around which the characters of *The Invasion* revolve. In essence, this manuscript is the image of the tragic situation of man, a symbol of what Richard Sherrell calls "the undiscernable meaning which invades life at its core."[11] Jean's papers represent the vain, disheartening quest for meaning in life. Pierre cannot determine what the man wrote, the handwriting is unclear—he cannot cope with the task and is unable to find his way out of the hopeless morass. Even if a sentence can be deciphered, it must be placed in the total context of the complete disorder of the papers; there is even the strong suggestion that if Pierre were to make some sense of the manuscript, the final answer might be absurd or meaningless.

In addition, these papers have become an invasion of Pierre's own life. In his determination to understand their meaning, he is spending his time on what has become an unreasonable project, an obsession. Adamov implies that the work is not meant to be deciphered and, more significantly, Pierre does not even plan to publish his results if he were able to complete the task. Thus, the playwright expresses the total futility of an exaggerated devotion to an idea which harms the individual involved and which is of no benefit to others. The idea of being obsessed with something to the point of not functioning adequately as a human being (a topic most pertinent to Adamov's own life) would be repeated by the dramatist in later plays, notably in *Le Ping-Pong*. At one moment, Pierre himself refers to this when he indicates his wish to lead a normal human existence again. Adamov thus seems to be pointing out that this quest for meaning (i.e., the obsession to decipher the manuscript) becomes a means of escape rather than a way of living one's life. It is a flight from reality, an attempt to cover up the difficulties of existence. The playwright also suggests that the manuscript's invasion of Pierre's life is reciprocated in turn by Pierre's own violation of Jean's past existence through his persistence in understanding the words of the dead writer. Jean wanted to destroy his own manuscript because it reminded him of what he had suffered—Pierre is thus the intruder in this world. It is in this context that we can understand Pierre's comment at the end of *The Invasion*, while tearing up the manuscript: "Pardon me for not having understood you earlier" (*Th.*, I, 93). It is also possible to interpret the sentence as an indication of Pierre's realization of the message which Jean might have wished to convey: the meaninglessness of everything, including the manuscript.

Pierre's work on the manuscript has been a series of frustrations and defeats, even more so because his life has been invaded on all levels, for all reasons: by his wife, who brings disorder; by his mother, who struggles with the wife for domination; by Tradel, who only adds imprecision to the difficult task of deciphering the manuscript; by the relatives of the dead man, who are suing over the use of the papers; by "the first one who comes along," who takes Agnès away. The audience is meant to see, in a concrete, physical manner, this intrusion into Pierre's personal world and the disorder that it has created. Following Artaud's concept of filling up space and Adamov's own desire to express verbal concepts through visual means, the playwright has indicated that the first sight the audience will see on the stage is the complete untidiness and disarray of items, the visual aspect expressing the disorder in the situation and in the mind of Pierre. This clutter is the image of Adamov's anguished cry of the artist's need to create in tranquillity as well as the human being's psychological demand for stability, a need which the dramatist never resolved in his own life. Agnès, who mirrors the role of Lili in the previous play, represents the first and major disorder in Pierre's household and the reason that he is unable to progress with his work. This confusion is then reflected in the use of language, which itself becomes more and more incomprehensible, seemingly disintegrating before Pierre's eyes, as he is unable to make any sense of what he is doing: "Why does one say, 'It happens'? Who is this 'it,' what does it want of me? Why does one say 'on' the ground, rather than 'at' or 'over'? I have lost too much time thinking about these things" (*Th.*, I, 86).

Yet, in this quest for normalcy, it is clear that order is not going to bring Pierre the peace of mind which he needs. With order comes the visible control of his mother, a control suggested on stage by her "voluminous" armchair, which becomes, little by little, the dominant, all-enveloping piece of furniture. Once the mother has rid the family of Agnès, the social fabric of the country has also rid itself of all of the "immigrants" who are crossing the border, an ironical twist which Adamov must have inserted while thinking of his own days as an immigrant and meditating on the narrow-mindedness of those people who are afraid of others who are different. And with order comes a sense of sterility and hopelessness, perhaps even more agonizing than that associated with disorder. Now that Agnès no longer has any use for him, and now that he discovers that the manuscript can no longer be used as a basis for deciphering some sort of sense in life, existence holds not even a minimal sort of meaning, and his only response is suicide. In this respect *The Invasion* reflects Adamov's ambivalence in his own life. While seeking a rational, stable, day-by-day life, the writer also recognized that the very elements which might cause the disorder and seemingly stifle creativity were those which were also most needed for an artist's development. To a great extent, Pierre needs Agnès in spite of the chaos which she may bring with her, because she also represents the very difficult, but necessary, world of human relationships. To attempt to be free of her, to rid oneself of human contact, particularly with a woman, is to deform the nature of the real world, in a sense to reenter the mother's womb. Such a situation is a flight from maturity and Pierre, like Adamov himself, can only find such psychological adjustments a frightening experience.

In expressing Pierre's awareness of the problems of human understanding, Adamov is continuing with the theme which he presented in *The Confession* and *The Parody*. In addition, in *The Invasion* the playwright thought that he had discovered a very effective means of representing the lack of communication between people: "I found it annoying that I, who had shown so well the impossibility of any conversation, was also obliged to write simple dialogues, just like anyone else. I then had recourse to a plan: yes, they [the characters] will speak, each one will hear what the other says, but the other will not be saying what he really has to say. In order to succeed in this plan, I desperately sought out key sentences which, apparently, would relate to daily life, but, basically, would mean 'something quite different'" (*Th.*, II, 9). The playwright wanted to stress that people are either incapable of or unwilling to express themselves directly on subjects, that conversation itself is a concealment of the real feelings of the individual. As a result, the characters in the play utilized what Adamov called "indirect dialogue." When Pierre asks Agnès if she will be able to continue working with him on the manuscript, it is also a very thinly-disguised effort to find out if she still loves him. At the end of Act V, Agnès returns, claiming that she needs to borrow the typewriter, an oblique statement of her wish to be accepted back by Pierre. Adamov later expressed his regret over the fact that his technique was not so original as he had first imagined: Chekhov, for one, had already made extensive use of this type of allusive dialogue as a basis of his theater.

The Invasion is a continuation of Adamov's personal ruminations on man's desperate plight: He is alone, confused, and afraid, the world is still a hostile enemy which he must confront each day. This second play by the dramatist is a much more successful expression of his ideas, for, while *The Parody* was a schematic, stylized representation, lacking any feeling of human warmth, *The Invasion* is a more complex and full-bodied work. In this work, the writer has developed characters who, while not having the consistency of those of the psychological theater, are nevertheless readily identifiable in their emotions and feelings. Although still used as symbols, they are no longer the almost lifeless figures of "N." and The Employee. Then too, the futile attempt to decipher the manuscript, symbolizing the hopelessness of the quest for meaning, provides the drama with a greater sense of life's tragedy. Because the play is dealing with comprehensible situations in a family milieu, the audience is able to respond more deeply to the sentiment of frustrated agony which the playwright wished to communicate. Furthermore, the piece retains the spectator's interest because it is obvious that Adamov the writer placed so much of himself in the character of Pierre. This strong sense of identification between character and author achieves the final effect of making Pierre a hero, almost a "positive" character, an infrequent occurrence at this stage in Adamov's writing. The dramatist later criticized what he had done, saying that it reminded him too much of the role of the hero in a Romantic drama like Alfred de Vigny's *Chatterton*. Nonetheless, much of the power of the work comes from the real emotion of despair which Adamov created in Pierre, a combination of frustration and fear—the playwright's own tortured response to life.

V   *The Disorder of Solitude:* Le Désordre (The Disorder)

In 1950, Adamov wrote a short and generally unimportant play called *Le Désordre (The Disorder)*, which was published in the first and only edition of the journal called *Eléments*.[12] The subject of the work, which has never been presented on stage, is a love triangle and, once again, the themes of solitude, lack of communication, and the difficulties of the male-female relationships are examined. In Adamov's words, the play is meant "to convey literally, physically, the disorder of spiritual isolation." He hoped to achieve this by the bareness of the setting and the solemn, slow performance of the actors.

Composed of ten brief scenes and divided into two parts, *The Disorder* tells the story of Simon, an architect, who is encountering financial difficulties in his business life. At the same time, his personal life is complicated by his jealousy over a relationship which has developed between his wife, Nina, and his friend, Laurent. In the second part of the play, Nina and Laurent have fled and are now living in an area somewhere on the outskirts of a city. They are leading a life of poverty; Laurent is seeking work but cannot find any. At this moment, "The Happiest of Women"[13] offers them lodging. However, the couple does not want to accept the offer from this woman who seems to be a mother figure, since the two people wish to retain their independence. Simon reappears in their lives and Nina eventually decides to return to him. After provoking a fight with Laurent, Simon strangles him. Nina places her head on Simon's shoulder, asking for pardon.

This curious play, with its melodramatic ending, evokes a little of the dreamlike atmosphere of *The Parody* and attempts to study the disorder of the emotional relationships of the characters. Once more, the woman is unstable in her dealings with men, moving from one to another. And, again, death is a final solution. This time, however, both men do not share the same final destiny as Simon presumably will return with his wife. As Pierre Mélèse notes in his work, "Adamov was wise in deciding not to include this minor work in his *Théâtre complet*."[14]

VI *The* Mutilé *and the* Militant:
La Grande et la Petite Manoeuvre
(The Great and the Small Maneuver)

At first glance, *La Grande et la Petite Manoeuvre (The Great and the Small Maneuver)* seems to be merely a reworking of Adamov's first two plays. The same basic idea reappears—all paths lead to destruction; the character types are similar and woman is again portrayed as a deceitful and indifferent manipulator of man. Upon closer inspection, however, it becomes evident that the playwright has further refined and improved his craft so that the content of the play, which closely parallels *The Parody*, is decidedly superior in its technical control and is consequently more effective in the exposition of its subject. Moreover, Adamov shows more directly than in his previous plays the major role of man's psyche in his life. And the social and political themes, which were part of the background in the first two works, are now important themes. As a result, *The Great and the Small Maneuver* (hereafter referred to as *The Maneuver*) may be listed as the dramatist's first political play, even though he later denounced its point of view.

After having completed *The Invasion*, Adamov still had the impression that he had not found a violent enough means to portray the powerlessness and impotence of man. A dream which he experienced during this period gave him the opportunity to pursue the theme further: "I was sitting on a wall facing the sea with my sister, or rather, a sister; I knew that, from one moment to the next, I was going to have to leave her to obey a call; somewhere, Monitors were waiting for me to impose terrible sessions on me relating to military training and gymnastics, sessions during which I would be mutilated, then destroyed, I was sure" (*Th.*, II, 10). In *Man and Child*, the writer elaborated further upon this dream: "I have to march in step, climb ropes, flatten myself on the ground, crawl; I am afraid" (*HE*, p. 95). He tells himself that he will not answer the voices of the Monitors, but he knows that he is lying—he will answer as soon as "they" call. Moreover, in the dream, his sister tells him: "You must go." And, to quote Adamov, "I always obey her." From this communication with his subconscious, the dramatist developed his play, in which a man loses the limbs of his body one by one after having obeyed the calls of unknown forces. What interested the playwright most strongly was that the dream had helped provide him with an effective theatrical expression of the emotion of fear, which he considered basic to human existence.

The Maneuver was the first play written by Adamov to be presented on the stage and he held a special remembrance of it, even though he later criticized its political theme. The piece was performed on November 11, 1950 at the Théâtre des Noctambules under the direction of Jean-Marie Serreau with Roger Blin performing the role of the *Mutilé*. Along with *The Invasion*, presented three days later by Jean Vilar, and *The Bald Soprano* of Ionesco, produced a few months before, the so-called theater of the absurd was beginning to make itself known. Adamov attended most of the rehearsals of *The Maneuver*, offering all the help that he could. Unfortunately, even with a decent reaction from the press, the play lasted only twenty-five performances. Roger Blin felt that the problem came from finding the proper style for performing Adamov: "It was difficult to find the right proportion of immediate realism and a certain style which keeps the dreamlike ambiguity that Adamov wanted."[15]

The Maneuver is a tightly-constructed play, paralleling the activities of the revolutionary leader, the *Militant*, who is waging a struggle against the brutal dictator of the country, and the *Mutilé*, who passively accepts control over his life from unseen Monitors who shout orders at him, causing him to lose each of his limbs. In both cases, Adamov wanted the spectator to understand that each person is defeated in advance, regardless of the path which he may have chosen. The theme is announced in the first tableau: The *Mutilé*, a terrified and helpless victim, is held by two police officers, while the *Militant*, being tortured in the wings, is thrown onto the stage, bloody and beaten. Arranged in ten short tableaux, the work alternates the activities of the two men. The path which the *Militant* has selected has led him to struggle against the police state, but he has neglected his family in the process. His wife, the *Mutilé*'s sister, criticizes her husband for not caring for her and for their sick child; they cannot get medicine for the child because of the very disorders created by the *Militant* and his group. Later, when the revolution has been successful, the new leader must leave his family again to speak to the people. Before departing, his child dies and his wife blames him for having caused the death. When he does deliver the speech to the crowd, it is clear that the revolutionaries have had to use methods in their rebellion which are as brutal as the police techniques, indicating that their cause is not without its own sordidness.

The *Mutilé*, on the other hand, is the helpless victim of the voices from the subconscious. These voices force him to obey to such an extent that he will place his hands into a machine which will cut them off, or he will throw himself under a car so that his leg is destroyed. In spite of these self-destructive acts, he tries to lead a normal life. While taking a course in typing for one-armed people (a

course which Adamov claimed he once saw advertised in a newspaper), he meets Erna, who seemingly takes an interest in him. Erna
becomes the possible means of his salvation from his voices, but,
like the other women in Adamov's theater, she betrays him, for,
while pretending to care for him, she is also the mistress of an agent
of the secret police. Nor does the *Mutilé*'s sister provide him with any
help. She has an almost incestuous need for him, complicating his
life further by her jealousy over his friendship with Erna. Thus, at
the end, the *Mutilé* is alone and weak, unable to control his life,
subject to the masochistic power of his subconscious, a helpless
victim in a car, both legless and armless.

The play is divided along the lines of the two major characters. In
a letter to Carlos Lynes, Adamov commented that the word *manoeuvre*, as he was using it, had a double meaning, referring to both
the military (hence, political) and the psychological.[16] "The Great
Maneuver" refers to the terror and fear which Adamov saw as the
main burden of the human condition and which he presented in the
drama of the *Mutilé*. "The Small Maneuver" concerns the particular
social and political injustices against which man must struggle, as
does the *Militant*. In both cases, the playwright demonstrates once
more that the end result is defeat and despair, whether one accepts
the passive state of the *Mutilé*, terrorized by his inner forces, or
whether one follows the activist trail of the revolutionary leader.
Whatever the choice, some sort of malevolent fate always provides
the same answer: futility, uselessness.

On the personal side, the *Mutilé* is certainly the character who
represents Adamov, a symbol of his masochistic obsessions. Besides
the passivity in the face of the seemingly unconquerable forces, the
Mutilé is also literally torn to pieces, limb by limb, during the course
of the play, a picture of Adamov's own feelings of disintegration and
deterioration. The helplessness of the *Mutilé* in the final scene is a
strikingly vivid portrait of the author's personal sense of physical
and emotional degeneration—impotent before the strength of his
own psychic forces which he cannot control. At the same time, the
character makes us think of the central figure in Kafka's *Metamorphosis,* who undergoes his own slow deterioration and disintegration.

Woman also plays her role in the *Mutilé*'s collapse by inflicting
pain and humiliation upon him. Erna (probably a name relating to
Adamov's friend, Irène, who nicknamed him "Ern"), represents
the dominance, cruelty, and capriciousness that the playwright saw

in the female. He again underscores the impossibility of love, mainly because of woman's inconstancy. It is Erna who appears to want the love of the *Mutilé*, but who gives herself to Neffer, the agent of the secret police. Whereas at one point she seems to offer the *Mutilé* the strength to continue, she then turns around and maliciously drags him down, just as the prostitutes used to crush Adamov with their spiked heels. Erna uses her psychological wiles ("What woman would want you? Except this poor imbecile Erna") and her physical superiority: At one moment, when he has only one leg, she pulls his crutches away from him and, after he falls, she adds, "Come on now, just try a little." It is also Erna ("You see, I must be kind to everybody. That's my work"), who, at the end of the play, kicks the cart in which the *Mutilé* is placed, pushing it offstage, saying, "Watch out. You could be crushed. You occupy so little space!" The playwright suggests that she has never been interested in the *Mutilé* for the purposes of love. Like the mother in *The Invasion,* she wants to control and dominate him. Even if she has a wish to aid him, it is less an act of charity or understanding than a realization that he is a helpless cripple whom she can manipulate.

In the cases of both the *Mutilé* and the *Militant,* Adamov points out that the inability to give or receive love is the cause of much of their trouble. Both men could be saved if they could make contact with another human being, particularly a woman, as seen in this plea by the *Mutilé*: "Erna! I beg you! Let me believe that you aren't completely indifferent to me. If I lose confidence once more, then . . . everything will begin again. Erna, we're dealing with my life. You must understand. All I have to do is to doubt you for a single moment and I will be forced to go off with 'them' once again" (*Th.,* I, 130). The theme of the incapacity for love is repeated over and over. While Erna crushes the *Mutilé* because of her lack of interest, he is unable to provide the necessary affection which his sister demands of him. And the *Militant* is also unable to give his desperately needed love to his wife and to his sick child. As Martin Esslin observes,

The categorical imperative that forces the *militant* to risk his life, to leave his wife in fear and trembling and ultimately to cause the death of his sick child, is shown as springing, basically, from the same inability to love as the implacable self-destructive commands of the subconscious mind that force the *mutilé* into masochistic self-destruction. The aggressive impulses of the *militant* are merely the reverse side of the *mutilé*'s aggression against himself.[17]

The Maneuver is not only a personal cry of anguish, but an attempt (although somewhat superficial) to present the theme of revolution and the struggle against social injustices. For the first time, Adamov turned to political situations as one of the bases of his theater. Although his later plays proclaim a Marxist philosophy, here Adamov is anti-Marxist. He is asking two fundamental questions: Is political action worth the loss of innocent lives? Do the means justify the ends? In both cases, his answer is "No." The *Militant* is shown as having foresaken his family for a cause that is as corrupt as the one which he is fighting. Adamov underscores this point in the ninth scene, as the *Militant* explains that the revolutionary forces have had to use reprehensible means in order to achieve their goals. After his explanation, he says that they will nevertheless be able to hold their heads high, but then physically contradicts the statement by collapsing into the arms of his supporters.

Because of his turn toward Marxism and Communism, the playwright later rejected the political aspect of the work, maintaining that he would never allow it to be presented again: "At that time, I was not only anti-Stalin, but anti-Soviet. I could not imagine any revolution that was not a betrayal. *The Great and the Small Maneuver* is a reactionary play" (*HE*, p. 99). Adamov further criticized the play because he felt that the role of the *Mutilé* had been an attempt on his part to justify himself for not having actively participated in the causes of the Left; it was also his impression that his attempt to link the personal and political in the play was ineffective to the point of awkwardness. He regretted the fact that, rather than demonstrating the failure of a specific revolution, he had chosen instead to show the failure of the idea of revolution in general, having taken material of a relative nature and having given it an absolute quality. Adamov worked to change this in the following plays, as he turned to a more specific, sometimes factually-oriented theater.

The playwright was more satisfied with the technical than with the political achievements of the work, and he specifically mentioned his pleasure at the rhythm of the piece, the exaggeration of the facts, and the almost cinematographic arrangement of the tableaux. The drama is well constructed, and the effectively contrasting scenes furnish a powerful expression of his theme. Even more significant is the fact that this play is one of the best illustrations of his view that the theater should be able to take ideas and feelings and translate them into concrete visual images. What he attempted, particularly in these earlier plays, was to show that theater should be the place where the visible and invisible worlds could meet and clash; he tried to make the theater the overt realization of the hidden, latent content of life, in such a way that "the manifestation of this content should literally, *concretely, corporally* coincide with the content itself."[18] In so doing, Adamov emphasized the visual, creating a "theater where the gestures, the attitudes, the very life of the body have the right to free themselves from the conventions of language, to go beyond psychological conventions, in a word, to go to the very limits of their deep meaning."[19] In the previous plays, he had made initial efforts at presenting this theory and now, in *The Maneuver*, the playwright attained even greater success in his attempt to translate the content into concrete visual expression. The feeling of mutilation, fear, and the sensation of disintegration are all vividly displayed in the progressive loss of limbs suffered by the *Mutilé*. The dismemberment of the man becomes a perfect, objective example of the shattering, subjective feeling of decay which Adamov himself was experiencing.

It is this innovative use of the stage that remains the most significant aspect of *The Maneuver* today. The dramatist was beginning to find himself more comfortable in his new profession and, although he never did totally succeed in conforming to the demands of the stage, he never ceased to make efforts to develop his own individualistic vision of theater.

VII   *The Revolt Against the "Others":* Le Sens de la marche (The Direction of the March)

Adamov's fifth play is an odd mixture of the old and the new: Some of the themes are tiresome in their familiarity (the terrifying force of others who control our lives, the inability to find love), some are fresher, more recent (the suggestion of revolt against those who dominate us). The work seems to have ended up being something slightly different from what the author had originally intended. While Adamov wrote the play with little new in mind to express, it also appears that he was succeeding somewhat in freeing himself from his neuroses—at least in his writing. The "hero," the character who represents the dramatist, rebels against the "others"; for the first time, the "hero" begins to bear the burden of personal responsibility.

Le Sens de la marche, which can be translated as *The Direction of the March*,[20] was written in 1951, in part during the rehearsals for *The Maneuver* and *The Invasion*. Understandably, Adamov's energies were directed toward the productions of the two plays rather than to the composition of this work. In addition, he interrupted his writing in order to transcribe a dream which he had had and which eventually became one of his most successful works, *Le Professeur Taranne*. As a result, *The Direction of the March* became an onerous task to the playwright, a chore in which he had lost interest. In *Man and Child*, he devoted only one sentence to its background: "1951. I finished my play, *The Direction of the March*, without any pleasure, a weak copy of *Professor Taranne*" (*HE*, p. 102). He also later criticized the piece for being simply a reworking of *The Maneuver*, but *The Direction of the March* and *Professor Taranne* have the distinction of being the first two Adamov works presented by Roger Planchon at Lyon. At that time, Planchon was a young director of a promising theatrical troupe and, with these productions, he commenced his friendship with Adamov and began to earn his reputation as the major director of the dramatist's plays.

The Direction of the March makes the point that life is nothing more than an endless series of repetitions. Henri, the central character, is confronted with a variety of situations in which a father figure dominates his existence. In the Prologue, which sets the pattern for the play, Henri's father stops him from leaving with two friends who plan to help in the revolutionary struggle for justice and social order. The father controls him to such an extent that Henri fears that he will end up like his sister, Mathilde, who is nothing but a servant to the father and to the father's sinister friend and *masseur*, Berne. Each succeeding act presents variations on the theme of authority exercised by paternal figures: the commanding officer in the barracks where Henri is completing his military service; the leader of a religious sect, who is also the father of Henri's fiancée, Lucile; and the headmaster of a school in which Henri is teaching (each one of the characters is played by the same actor who performs the role of Henri's father). Throughout the four segments, Henri submits to the authority above him while, at the same time, he is mocked and scorned by others around him: the soldiers at camp, those who participate in the religious sect, and the students in the schoolroom. He finally returns home, seemingly broken in spirit. But when he discovers that Berne has taken over his dead father's home, even to the point of perhaps being his sister's lover, Henri revolts and strangles him.

Adamov has explained what he considered the central theme of the play in these terms: "In this life, in which the basic circumstances are horrible, in which situations inevitably repeat themselves, all we can do is destroy, and too late at that, what we consider mistakenly to be the real obstacle, but what is merely the last in an evil series (Henri's murder of the *masseur*, Berne, the false father)" (*Th.*, II, 11–12). In this endless maze of frustration and confusion called life, Adamov's idea that we strike back at the world but often mistake our target is inventive. Yet, there is another more interesting aspect of the work: Like the *Militant* in *The Maneuver*, the central figure rebels against forces controlling him, counterattacking against authority, suggesting that the dramatist may have achieved some progress in coping with his own tyrannical forces. And, for the first time, one central character represents the two sides of Adamov, for he is both the victim and the rebel.

Basically, the playwright shows that those who have authority tend to destroy rather than to develop. Tradition, suggests Adamov, that stalwart of societies, has aborted many revolutionary, hence creative, developments in the course of history. This type of restrictive control, often found in the family in the parent-child relationship, is even more widespread: It is also present in the submission required by the army, the devotion demanded by religion, and the order established in the schools. The dramatist again raises the question of the conflict of disorder and order, with an implicit appeal for disorder. All those who require order—the father, the Commander, the headmaster of the school—are responsible for limiting the growth of the individual. Mathilde, Henri's sister, is shown as a pitiful example of one who has no choice but to follow the path set up by those in command; she is nothing more than a slave. The continual parade of followers who surround those in power are depicted as crude and insensitive to anyone who does not fit their pattern of conformity. They are lifeless characters, with no individuality—the same actors play the roles of the followers in each situation. Woman, besides being a cause of man's inability to find love, now also becomes another source of the stifling of man's independence; Henri's fiancée Lucile has, in her own way, worked against his revolutionary activities. It is because of her as much as his father that Henri does not leave with the rebels, going so far as to submit to the control of the Sect and Lucile's father so that he can be near her. And it is because Henri doubts Lucile's fidelity to him that he has a fight with Georges, one of the leaders of the revolution, thus ending his association with the movement.

Henri also appears to be the typical Adamovian figure in this early part of the dramatist's writing: He has a masochistic guilt feeling, accompanied by paranoia about the "others" who are mocking him, as well as a tendency to justify and to excuse his weaknesses by blaming someone else. At one point, Henri talks about joining the revolutionaries: "Of course, I could still leave, there is still time. They will always want me. There are not so many men ready to sacrifice themselves. The offer remains open. Only, I am broken and I no longer believe in it [the revolutionary movement]! It's not my fault. *They* are responsible! All of them! They have won" (*Th.*, II, 55). Nevertheless, we find indications for the first time that the central character (hence, Adamov) is becoming aware of his responsibility and will accept some of the burden which life has placed upon him, suggesting that the theater was also helping the playwright to come to terms with his neuroses. Henri has intermittent realizations of his accountability: his feelings of guilt transcend mere masochism and are realistically directed at himself for having failed to take some form of inner and outer control of his life. While speaking to his students, Henri states what is essentially the theme of the work, although Adamov chose to ignore the subject in his own comments on the play. Like the speech of the *Militant* in *The Maneuver*, Henri's lecture to the class is in contradiction to his own life. The aimless Henri, controlled by others, tells his class: "It's not difficult, however. I'm not asking you to recite my sentences by heart, mechanically. If you make a mistake, if you forget something, that doesn't make any difference. Provided that you give the meaning, provided that you state the goal" (*Th.*, II, 52). In this context, we see the direction of Adamov's thinking as he begins to consider the importance of action, particularly social and political action. The title of the play, *The Direction of the March*, is a clear indication that the playwright feels that each individual should have some sort of purpose to his existence. As Henri mentions to his students: "When you don't have any goal, when you don't aim constantly at the same precise point, then you yourself become the target" (*Th.*, II, 52). What is significant about Adamov's position is that the personal, masochistic guilt feelings of *The Confession* and the previous plays are beginning to disappear. Henri is guilty not because of some indefinable reason, but because he has not taken some control over his life, and the final act shows that he is willing to take concrete steps to remedy the situation.

In Act IV, Henri refuses to submit to Berne and strangles him. In this symbolic action there is the first real revolt against authority, against tradition, the first sense of direction. While it is true as Adamov pointed out that the revolt is not directed against the original source of the problem (in this case, the father), it is nonetheless also true that the rebellion takes place against someone who represents the same, and perhaps even more individious, type of authority; and Henri is now aware of and willing to accept the burden of his actions. He is no longer the confused, indecisive character of *The Invasion*, whose only solution was suicide. Rather, Henri's response reflects the existential attitude of Jean-Paul Sartre: act, perform the gesture which will direct your life.

In the final analysis, however, it would be a mistake to think that this play represented a major and significant change on the part of the dramatist. If we can believe his comments, he did not even consider the themes of responsibility and revolt to be important in this work, and we find a decidedly ambiguous attitude toward the value of Henri's action. It could be interpreted that Henri's final revolt developed from frustration and not from any real desire to take positive action. The revolution itself is presented so vaguely and with such little substance that we cannot understand why Henri should be eager to involve himself in it. Adamov recognized this weakness: "One would have to believe in this aborted revolution, and certainly the appearances of Georges and Albert could never make it convincing" (*Th.*, II, 12). In fact, at times, the parallels between Georges and Albert, the two revolutionaries in the play, and the voices of the Monitors in *The Maneuver* are so striking that it is possible that Adamov meant to draw a similarity.

The Direction of the March is one of the least successful of Adamov's plays, principally because it seems to have become something other than what the playwright had intended. The most striking features remain the central figure's awareness of responsibility and his turn toward action as a solution to problems, even though this was not the dramatist's purpose. Unlike most of the other plays which Adamov wrote, he made no particular attempt to experiment with special visual or verbal devices, nor did he take special efforts to perfect the drama, since his interest in the work was minimal. In fact, the play reads as well as it performs, having been constructed in a fairly traditional manner, a rarity in Adamov's theater.

VIII   *The Struggle with the Inner and Outer Worlds:*
Le Professeur Taranne (Professor Taranne)

In 1951, while in the midst of rehearsals for *The Maneuver* and *The Invasion*, and while writing *The Direction of the March*, Adamov also composed what may well be his most successful play, *Le Professeur Taranne (Professor Taranne)*. This work is an almost literal transcription of a dream which he had had, and the composition took two days and three nights, as compared to the total of five years which his first two plays had required.

Professor Taranne, a one-act drama in two scenes, is one of Adamov's richest and most rewarding works. The familiar theme is again presented—the absurdity, futility, and fear of existence—but this time, compared to his previous plays, the writing is more direct, the emotions more identifiable, and the structure more cohesive. In his notes, the playwright pointed out the strength of the work: "*Professor Taranne* was, for me, a significant event, because, for the first time, I simply transcribed a dream without trying to bestow on it a general sense, without wanting to prove anything, without adding any intellectual exoneration to that probably contained in the dream itself" (*Th.*, II, 12). This direct expression of the subconscious feelings of the dramatist is a major factor in the play's appeal and was also the reason that Adamov still preferred the work a few years after having written it: "If *Professor Taranne* satisfied me and still satisfies me, it is because I did not use any of the elements of my dream for allegorical purposes. . . . It is also, at least in part, because I did not seek to guide the speeches of Taranne: I let him speak, as I probably spoke myself in the dream" (*Th.*, II, 13). As a result, the play became for Adamov a deeper, hence, more moving realization of his concerns. The dream provided him with the opportunity to explore his relationship to the inner and outer worlds (the areas of the subconscious and external reality) and to pursue the question of man's identity.

First presented along with *The Direction of the March* at the Théâtre de la Comédie in Lyon on March 18, 1953 by Roger Planchon,[21] the play deals with man's inability to cope with the hostile forces outside and within him. Professor Taranne has been accused by some children of indecent exposure on a beach. He denies the charge, stating that he is a distinguished scholar who has been invited to give courses abroad, particularly in Belgium; he is sure that people who know him will attest to his morality. However, the more he proclaims his innocence, the more doubtful his story becomes. At the police station, a lady journalist confuses him with another professor, Ménard, and two acquaintances of the journalist also claim that they do not recognize Taranne.

In the second scene, at Taranne's hotel, two policemen now charge him with having left paper lying about in the bathing cabin at the seaside where he had changed his clothes. Taranne protests that he did not take a cabin that day, thereby unwittingly confirming the previous charge that he had changed his clothes in public. The two policemen also produce a notebook which they have found. Taranne recognizes it as his, but cannot read it, as the pages are written in a handwriting which he does not know. In addition, only the first and last pages of the book have any writing on them, although the professor maintains that he filled the book up completely. He then receives a large roll of paper, containing the seating plan of a dining room of a ship on which he has supposedly booked passage, but which only mystifies him further, as he maintains he knows nothing about this. His sister Jeanne arrives with a letter from the Rector of the University of Belgium where he gave his courses. The letter informs him that he will not be rehired because of incompetency and because he plagiarized his lectures from Professor Ménard. At this point, Professor Taranne hangs the roll of paper on the wall and it is completely blank. With his back to the audience, he looks at the paper and then, slowly, begins to undress, performing the very act of which he has been accused.

The dream and its expression in the play are further evidences of Adamov's neuroses: his masochism, seen in Taranne's humiliation when he begins to disrobe, and his paranoia, as noted in Taranne's persecution by the children, the police, those who fail to recognize him, and the Rector of the University. In addition, besides these familiar areas of concern, new insecurities occurred in the playwright's psychological makeup, ironically enough caused by his writing. At the time that Adamov experienced this nightmare, he was involved with the rehearsals for *The Maneuver* and *The Invasion*, and he had also just had his first two plays published. As a result, this initial public exposure created deep feelings of uneasiness, as Adamov commented in his notes: "Everything that happens in the play to the professor happened to me in the dream, with the difference that, instead of crying out, to prove my 'honorability': 'I am Professor Taranne,' I cried out: 'I am the author of *The Parody*!' The result was not, moreover, any better" (*Th.*, II, 12). Just as Taranne did not measure up to what he was supposed to be, it would appear that Adamov had doubts about his ability to live up to his role as a writer.[22] Even more than that, the play expresses the dramatist's fear of not being recognized or appreciated in his adopted country: "*Professor Taranne*, a symptomatic text. My fear of being nothing more than a lecturer, a traveling salesman, an author invited abroad, ignored in France" (*HE*, p. 101). Taranne is the symbol of what might happen to Adamov if, as he saw it, his literary talents were not properly appreciated in France. It is also clear that the blank pages in the notebook are an indication of the playwright's fear that his work lacks real merit or value, the journalist who does not recognize him symbolizes the dramatist's concern that he will suffer literary obscurity, and the accusation of plagiarism reflects his doubts over the originality of his works.[23]

In Adamov's view, *Professor Taranne* has considerable importance in his progress and development as a playwright for, paradoxically, this transcription of a dream allowed him to approach the real world. For the first time, he noted, he had named an actual place, Belgium, and he had spoken of a letter coming from that country, bearing a stamp with the Royal Lion on it: "That seems like nothing, but it was all the same the first time that I emerged from a pseudo-poetic *no-man's-land* and dared to call things by their name" (*Th.*, II, 13). It was Adamov's contention that this first contact with reality in his theater was a significant factor in leading him to the more concrete realities of his later plays.

It must be admitted that *Professor Taranne* would contain very little if it were limited to these quite personal obsessions of the author. Since it is not, this play is probably the one Adamovian work with which the public can most readily identify. The piece contains nothing extraneous, each part being closely integrated to the whole; the steady, almost logical progression leading to Taranne's disrobing and his defeat at the hands of the world is effectively constructed, starting with the original charge against the professor, followed by a merciless disintegration, bit by bit, of his facade of respectability.

Like the progressive dismemberment of the *Mutilé* in *The Maneuver*, Taranne is left, in his own way, a helpless cripple at the end. And the inevitability of this constant movement toward his destruction makes a highly trenchant statement about man at the mercy of fate. The situation also recalls once again Kafka's *Metamorphosis* and the situation of the man in *The Trial* who is arrested for a crime of which he is completely unaware.

The effect of this structure is such that Adamov is extremely successful in capturing and placing on stage the emotion of fear, the basis of all of his works. The fear that Adamov is telling us about is really, as Carlos Lynes calls it, "the drama of a man's inner dispossession."[24] The play is meant to be an exposition of the slow but steady erosion of man's inner defenses, his internal security, his inability to live up to the role which the outer world expects of him. When Taranne turns to others for support of his claims, he is rejected and his world is torn apart. After having proclaimed that the students find his lectures excellent, he is informed by the Rector: "They tell me finally that the attention of your listeners fell off considerably, that some went so far as to speak out loud, and that others left the lecture hall before you had finished" (*Th.*, I, 234). When he is confronted with the charges made by the children, or with the notebook which seems to be his but which he cannot read, Taranne cannot help but question his own acts, doubt his own sanity, and submit to the terror which the contradictions between the outer and inner worlds have created within him.

The reason that the playwright has succeeded so well in this play as opposed to his previous works is that the protagonist, Professor Taranne, is a purposely ambiguous, complex, rich creation. In the earlier plays, the dramatist had often composed schematic, almost diagrammatical works around allegorical characterizations, in which the figures were lifeless and the dramas cold and mechanical. *Taranne* is much less clear-cut in its intentions: Is the central character a celebrated scholar as he claims? Or is he a fraud, who plagiarizes the works of others? Did he actually undress on the beach? Or is this simply an accusation made by some fanciful children? Out of this ambiguity, Adamov has created his most fascinating characterization, approaching a creation of more than one dimension, although still far removed from the characterizations of the traditional psychological theater. As Maurice Regnaut points out, Adamov's dream allowed the playwright to fuse the two seemingly contradictory attitudes of his previous plays into one single character,[25] a technique which the playwright had begun to develop in *The Direction of the March*. In the early works, in order to demonstrate that life is futile and absurd, ending in nothingness, Adamov had to turn to two characters, each endowed with different life styles. In *Professor Taranne*, the protagonist possesses both aspects simultaneously: He is passive and active, constructive and destructive at the same time. At the very moment that he is telling us of his achievements as a scholar and human being, he is also contradicting these statements. It is not clear—and it is not meant to be clear—if he is innocent or guilty of the charges leveled against him, or if he is or is not the distinguished professor he claims to be. In Adamov's nightmarish world, in which nothing is ever what it seems to be, where ostensibly ordinary objects become forces of hostility, where life is a complex turmoil of unanswered, perhaps unanswerable questions, the emotions of the character of Taranne, with their conflicting, often opposing, qualities, are very much alive. By means of ambiguity and by ascribing contradictory but basically human qualities to Taranne, Adamov has created his most recognizable character, paradoxically an achievement of his subconscious.

In point of fact, the subconscious is the motivating force in the whole work. The nightmare which Adamov experienced and turned into theatrical form was a demand from the subconscious that Adamov, the human being, come to terms with his inner and outer realities and find a stable, mature identification for himself. Throughout the play-dream, the spectator is never able to decipher what is real and what is imaginary because the protagonist himself does not know. The claims of the professor are immediately answered and contradicted by the supposed reality around him. This reality of the outer world is cruel and heartless in its "truth," and Taranne, like Adamov, cannot deal with it. Taranne is speaking to the Inspector and his associate when he discovers that they have left without his being aware of it: "I would like to ask you if you have seen the Inspector or one of the employees . . . It's very annoying. I was supposed to sign my declaration . . . and . . . I haven't done it . . . (Terrified.) Nevertheless, they couldn't have left, one of us would have seen them. I don't understand . . ." (*Th.*, I, 225).[26] This almost illusory reality is pictured as a deadening, awesome force which conquers man, leaving him totally destroyed. At the end of the play, Adamov explains in his directions that the stage will remain empty, most of the scenery and props having been removed. The only items left are the notebook (an indication of the value of Taranne's work and the possibility of plagiarism), the letter (which recounts his failure as a teacher), and the roll of paper ("a large, grey, uniform surface, absolutely empty"). Reality has also left Taranne with the charge made by the children on the beach. Faced with this nothingness, except for his clothes, Taranne has no choice but to divest himself of those, too, accepting his defeat. In this respect, it is possible to view the ending as a sort of death, although symbolic this time. Taranne has not been able to avoid the failure which all the other Adamovian characters have suffered, because he has not been able to handle the real world.

Yet, paradoxically, it is also possible that there is a measure of hope in this final scene. In his desire to disrobe and reveal himself naked to the world, Taranne may very well be taking the first step toward a direct contact with himself and with the universe around him. Adamov's dream seems to state that man lives by an outer layer of respectability which constitutes his identity, his "reality." Once this layer is removed, what remains? What is left of the individual personality when the façade is destroyed? Although man is afraid to face this question, the playwright's dream would suggest that this is precisely what he must do. Besides the fear of coping with the outer world, Taranne is also afraid to cope with himself. The dream and the play call for a search for one's own reality hidden behind the mask of respectability, a realization of one's true identity. The dream is the attempt by the subconscious to find an accommodation between the inner and outer realities.

Because of the uncertainty of who is right, the professor or the people around him, and because of the playwright's own obvious sympathies for his central figure, the spectator is probably not meant to assume that Taranne must simply accept the "reality" of the outer world. The implication is made that the truth of any situation is found only in a coordination, a compromise of one's inner being with the outer world. Adamov's subconscious was asking him to find within himself the ability to master his obsessions and to function within the difficult realm of normal, everyday life, while still finding his own unique identity.

It is therefore understandable that Adamov should see *The Direction of the March* as a copy of *Professor Taranne*. Henri's revolt against his tormentors is Adamov's conscious reply to his subconscious; he will act, he will do something about his life. However, as the playwright has noted, *The Direction* was written to prove a point and it is because of that that the play suffers. *Taranne* is a fairly literal transcription of the dramatist's most personal fears, dictated by the subconscious. As such, it is an honest and relatively direct expression of a tortured soul. *Professor Taranne* is a powerful play and is the one work written by Adamov which communicates the sense of inner sadness as effectively as *The Confession*.

IX   *The Art of Persecution:*
Tous contre tous (One Against Another)

At this point in his career, Adamov was beginning to achieve prominence as a playwright. Three of his original plays had been performed as well as some of his adaptations, both on stage and on the radio. While some critics did not appreciate his individualistic approach, he was nevertheless being considered seriously as one of the important dramatists of the new, avant-garde theater. Having attained a measure of recognition, he was invited to theater festivals in Germany and Italy. Although money still remained a problem, there were periods, while working at a radio station in Stuttgart, when he thought of himself as "almost rich." Most important, he had also found a certain stability in his emotional life through his attachment to the *Bison*, Jacquie, who later became his wife.

As his life took on a semblance of structure and as his theater performed the function that he had hoped it would (helping to liberate him from his neuroses), Adamov felt less a need to present only his personal obsessions in his plays. While still including the familiar themes, his next work, *Tous contre tous (One Against Another)*, assigns a new importance to the political and social concerns of the dramatist. *One Against Another* is about persecution—man's persecution of his fellowman as well as the persecution by the powerful and moneyed of the powerless and the outcast.

The play commences with the sociopolitical theme: A radio announcer reports that social disturbances of unknown origins are plaguing the country. The blame is placed upon the refugees from abroad, who are readily identifiable because they all limp. Jean Rist, the protagonist, loses his job and attributes his misfortune to the influx of immigrants. He next loses his wife, Marie, to Zenno, one of the refugees whom Jean had previously helped when Zenno was being attacked by others. Zenno is now important because he has a specialty that the government needs. However, for a brief time, the situation changes and Jean assumes some of the power, vowing revenge on all the immigrants. Marie tries to help Zenno escape from the country and is killed herself in the process. Then, once more, the tide turns and Jean becomes the persecuted, rather than the persecutor. On the advice of his mother, he assumes a limp and pretends to be one of the refugees. His life remains quiet and he finds a certain contentment in his love for Noémi, a refugee. When there is another upheaval in this unstable world and the immigrants are once again persecuted, Jean can escape death only by revealing his true identity. Yet he refuses to do so because of his love for Noémi. At the same time, Jean's mother, who has a natural limp but is not one of the refugees, is killed along with the others because of her superficial resemblance to them. Finally, Zenno, who has official papers which will save him, offers himself to the guards and is also put to death, as one of the guards calls out, "All the same!"

One Against Another was performed on April 14, 1953, at the Théâtre de l'Oeuvre directed by Jean-Marie Serreau, who had also worked on *The Maneuver*. The critical reaction was generally quite favorable, mainly because, as one reviewer noted, the work is "the clearest and most direct of the plays of Adamov."[27] Other critics commented on the tighter structure of his theater and the use of a language that was more immediately comprehensible to the audience. Gabriel Marcel even went so far as to state that he preferred the play to Samuel Beckett's *Waiting for Godot*, an opinion which seems debatable in retrospect.[28]

Ostensibly, Adamov intended once again to pursue the theme of the desolation of life, this time, however, dealing with persecution on both a personal and a political basis. Although the persecution and torture of the refugees (who symbolize the Jews or the issue of racism in general) form the outer structure of the drama, the play has much in common with his previous efforts. As Geneviève Serreau observes, the work "is dominated by another more terrifying torture, with all its metaphysical implications: the torture of living which was already a part of the central characters of *The Parody*".[29] In this respect, the play is fairly routine, since the dramatist has already made the point so often before and, as in a case like *Professor Taranne*, so much better. Adamov again returns to his earlier structural pattern with two characters to represent man's struggle against a hostile world, ending in defeat. This time, though, the two characters, Jean Rist and Zenno, alternate in an up-and-down pattern between having power and being victimized outcasts; all that awaits either of them is death. The play begins and ends with the same words: *Tous les mêmes*! (All the same!), a point which Jean makes to his mother:

THE MOTHER. . . . But they want our death, your death, Jeannot. (*She twists her hands.*) Oh! I knew that it would end badly.
JEAN. It ends as it began. That's normal.
THE MOTHER. This isn't the moment to philosophize! They are going to come, Jeannot! And take you away! Take us away! We have to . . . we have to . . . do something quickly, quickly . . . In any case, we're not going to wait for them!
JEAN. Why not? Each one has his turn. (*Th.*, I, 189)

This same feeling of impotence and defeatism is echoed by Zenno, when he tells Marie to leave him and to return to Jean, now that the political wheels of fortune have changed: "You would be happier with him than with me. Times have changed. You can't do anything about the times in which you live. We are quite weak" (*Th.*, I, 172).

Adamov's choice of the mother as a central figure gives further evidence of his recourse to his normal themes. The mother again remains a dominant, too powerful influence on the personal life of the son. Like the mother of *The Invasion*, she detests the disorder and social upheaval which surround her, and she longs for a sense of stability and, hence, control. However, Adamov provides the mother in *One Against Another* with some subtle additions. She is now depicted as being as corrupt as those in power and she attempts to instill her practices in her son. The mother tells Jean that the only thing that counts is money and it is through money that man achieves his strength (undoubtedly a remembrance of the poverty-stricken childhood of Adamov, the refugee). She also encourages him to succeed in whatever way he can, even if it is by gross forms of deceit. It is the mother who urges him to adopt a limp so that he may escape harm when the refugees return to power. But Adamov now uses the mother-son relationship in a new, perhaps more liberating manner: Jean reacts against the mother, even to the point of physically striking her. This revolt again is only short-lived, since, as Jean notes bitterly, he can never escape her.

In *One Against Another*, Adamov presents an even more pessimistic view of the human condition than in previous writings. The law of self-preservation is the only guiding force. As George E. Wellwarth mentions, the play is basically "a microcosmic view of treachery, hate and double-dealing."[30] Both Jean and Zenno are alternately persecutor and persecuted. When Jean has a brief moment of control, his only thought is for revenge on all the refugees: "Rich and poor, all the same! All ready to take your bread, to lie in wait for your wives. . . . If I ask that you strike out at all the refugees without distinction, it is . . . it is in order to return your honor to you" (*Th.*, I, 164). In a similar manner, when Zenno has an opportunity to save himself by betraying Jean to those in power, he does not hesitate, even though it was Jean who had originally rescued him from his persecutors. Thus Adamov emphasizes his view that humanity will perform unspeakable acts and that these same acts are then reflected in our social system, which is simply an extension of human nature. In that respect, all mankind is indeed the same—and no hope remains.

It is perhaps because Adamov insists too strongly on this general consideration of man's inhumanity to his fellowman that the play does not succeed as well as it might. In view of his background as an émigré from Russia, and in view of his imprisonment at the beginning of World War II, it is obvious that the topic of persecution of the refugee must have been quite close to the playwright. But he fails to come to grips with the problem with which he is dealing. Essentially, although the piece is political and social as its title attests, it is diluted by the dramatist's insistence on making his personal obsessions once again the major theme. In his comments on the play, the dramatist recognized this weakness: "With *One Against Another*, once again I fell into the error, partially at least, that I had committed with *The Great and the Small Maneuver*: showing The Persecution instead of a persecution" (*Th.*, II, 13). Adamov felt that he should have created a work in a specific time and place about the Jews, for the work is fundamentally an allegory of the persecution of this minority: "Thus, I would have revealed, in a theatrical manner, a real, social mechanism, instead of reaching a conclusion which was, at the very least, hasty: 'All the same!'" (*Th.*, II, 14). He was satisfied, however, with the idea of creating the limp as an external indication, a literal representation of the hidden motives for the persecution.

While Adamov had never specifically commented on the inspiration for his play, he recounted an incident in *Man and Child* which bears a strong similarity to Jean Rist's situation. In 1941, when the writer was in the concentration camp in Argelès, the Germans did not want any Jews in their country and those who were in France or elsewhere were to remain there. Adamov, who was not Jewish but who wished to remain in France, had an idea, dictated by the fear that he would be deported: He would pass himself off as Jewish. He spoke to two German officials, who knew that he was lying and laughed derisively. But he insisted:

—"O.K., you think that I am not Jewish, but you can still put on the papers that I am. What does it matter to you?"
—The two German inspectors looked at each other: "You really want us to put the word 'Jewish' on your papers?"
—"Yes."
—The two German inspectors laughed heartily and hit their thighs. They clearly took me for a madman. "O.K. You will stay in France."
—They kept their word. (*HE*, pp. 69–70)

Adamov later learned that they had never stamped anything on his papers, but he was not sent out of the country. Whether this incident actually inspired the playwright or whether, once having thought of the idea for the drama, this seemed like a suitable addition to the work, it is not known. In any event, the story is an essential part of the play as Jean Rist chooses a similar method to save himself.

While Adamov was writing about persecution, he was also writing about unified, concerted action: The play is, in a minor and preliminary way, a revolutionary call for the unity of the oppressed against those in power. It is thus easy to see the future direction of the dramatist's theater. While those who limp are persecuted, the others, like Jean Rist, also suffer because they are likewise the pitiful, powerless prey of the ruling classes, represented in the play by Darbon. All men without power are victims at one time or another. The playwright has simply taken his basic neurosis—the virtual paranoia that made him see himself and all mankind as helpless pawns of fate—and he now links this neurosis to the political and social structure. The forces that control our lives will no longer be simply the irrevocable hand of fate or the dictates of the subconscious; they will now have a sociopolitical basis as well. The dramatist was beginning to move his attention from those forces about which he could do nothing to those upon which he could effect some change. He now stresses the exploitation of the persecuted by the rulers, who play both sides against each other, manipulating both with cruel ease. While each side sells out to the ruling class in order to obtain its small share of power, Adamov makes it clear that the real authority stays with those in power.

The political and social conflict of the play is, however, only partially developed and the work is not a full expression of Adamov's ideas. He seems to have shied away from this direct contact with reality, a flaw which he realized: "Jean Rist is a failure who is avenging himself. But, why is he a failure, and why is he avenging himself? Darbon, whose speeches I still appreciate—all you have to do is to open certain newspapers to find them—is the 'gentleman' who survives all regimes. But, what does he obey? What interests does he serve?" (*Th.*, II, 14). The dramatist also criticized the number of "good" and innocent victims to be found on the side of the refugees. Wanting to show that all sides were reprehensible (a position which his obvious sympathies belied), he felt that he had betrayed his intentions.

It would seem, though, that Adamov overlooked one of the more interesting facets of the play. For the first time in his world of despair and desolation, one finds a faint glimmer of hope for mankind in the characters of Noémi and The Worker. Noémi, Jean's friend, is an obviously honest and decent human being, whose understanding and loyalty provide the protagonist with a feeling of love, a sentiment missing from all of the dramatist's previous works. And the very brief appearance of The Worker foreshadows the "noble" characters to be found in *Le Printemps 71*. The Worker speaks with the voice of reason when he tells another man who still wants to continue the struggle against the immigrants by attacking Jean: "Imbecile! Those who are doing us harm are better rigged out than that. . . . Leave him alone. He is not any happier than we are" (*Th.*, I, 193). Adamov suggests that The Worker understands man's real situation, that the solution is to be found in unity, not divisiveness, a point which the playwright would develop in later plays.

We can now clearly see Adamov's admiration for the downtrodden of humanity, the "people," as reflected in the ending of the play which displays an almost sentimental and romantic faith in mankind. Because of his love for Noémi, Jean refuses to state that he does not limp and, as a result, he must go to his death; Zenno finally gives up his right to safety and allows himself to be revealed in his true identity as a refugee, also ready to face death. In these two self-sacrificing decisions, made out of honor, dignity, or love, Adamov appears to have taken a first positive step toward contact with his fellowman.

Before we decide that the playwright has made a major change in his approach to life and theater, however, it ought to be noted that there are other, less idealized interpretations of the ending. Martin Esslin sees Jean's refusal to save himself as "an act of resignation; of suicide in the face of an absurd, circular destiny." [31] Jean would then simply be displaying the same sense of self-destruction that all the previous characters have shown. Also, Geneviève Serreau raises the interesting possibility that Adamov became aware that he had made Zenno too unpleasant and that the dramatist himself risked the possibility of being called anti-Semitic, which was definitely contrary to his intentions. Therefore, she reports, Adamov changed the ending of the play: In an earlier version, Zenno escapes from his persecutors up to and including the end. [32] Indeed, it is very possible that this practical aspect prompted the change rather than the playwright's faith in mankind.

One Against Another is a transitional work. Adamov was still not out of the no-man's-land of his neuroses and personal obsessions, and he had still not moved into the strongly political vein of his later theater. The playwright was aware of this problem: "I suffered from the limitation imposed on me by the vagueness of the place, the schematization of the characters, the symbolism of the situations, but I did not feel the strength to take up the subject of social conflict, and to see it, as such, detached from the world of archetypes" (*Th.*, II, 14).

X *Regression to Childhood:*
Comme nous avons été (As We Were)
and Les Retrouvailles (The Reunions)

In *Comme nous avons été (As We Were)*, written around 1951 but published in 1953, and *Les Retrouvailles (The Reunions)*, written in 1954 and published in 1955, Adamov returned to a completely personal theater, eliminating all political references. Although written a few years apart, both works have much in common and represent an effort on the playwright's part to come to direct terms with his personal problems. Besides the dreamlike atmosphere with its structural arrangement involving confusion of time and place, the plays have a similar theme: a man's futile struggle against his family to obtain independence and maturity. Previously, the family had been a part of the whole, sometimes as much a victim as the writer, although in works like *The Invasion, One Against Another*, and *The Direction of the March*, the dramatist very decidedly pointed out his conflicts with family authority. At this juncture, however, he saw the whole question of his guilt, remorse, and responsibility deriving from and revolving around the family circle. In this sense, the fact that the playwright named a specific *human* cause for his psychological troubles was a major step forward; he did not use the intangible struggle of man against impersonal hostile forces. And, by the time that he wrote *The Reunions*, Adamov had reached the close of the first phase of his writing and the last time until the end of his career that he felt the need to use the theater primarily as a catharsis for his neuroses.

Basically, both *As We Were* and *The Reunions* deal with the issue of accepting the responsibility of adulthood, coping as a mature person in the real world. The two plays are built around the same structure—a grown man's regression to childhood just as he is about to achieve a sense of maturity through marriage. Adamov now attacks the mother directly, for she is responsible for the son's inability to establish an adult relationship with another human being, particularly with a woman; the mother who, by her possessive, harmful control, renders the son helpless, an impotent object. While Adamov, through "A." and Edgar, the characters who represent him, still tries to justify himself, it is also evident to the audience that the two protagonists are deluding themselves and that much of the responsibility for their difficulties must also lie with them.

As We Were was published in the *Nouvelle Nouvelle Revue Française* in March, 1953.[33] Adamov repudiated the work and it has never been placed in the Gallimard editions of his collected plays. In the drama, "A." is taking a nap in his room, sleeping in his evening clothes since he is about to leave to be married. Henriette appears, awakening him, in search of a little boy who was playing ball in the corridor and who may have wandered in to talk to him. Henriette, who is soon joined by the boy's aunt, tells "A." that the youngster is called André (bearing the same first initial as "A."). However, "A." is not interested in their problems and is openly hostile to their presence, almost as if he were afraid to hear what they had to say. Little by little, though, they enter his world through their persistent questioning. Although "A." is about to marry, it is evident that he has not yet stabilized his life. Following the relentless interrogation of the two women, he responds: "What do you want to know? If I'm earning a living? Well, no, not yet. But that's nothing special. I don't have any urgent need at the moment. Moreover, I'm not going to rush into anything, just to do something . . . just to give myself the impression of living, as they say today."[34] But he now has to face marriage and this will be difficult.

The two women begin to tell stories of their family life and "A." becomes interested in spite of himself. In fact, "A." seems to be familiar with these tales, as he often intervenes and completes them himself. In this highly autobiographical part of the play, Adamov has drawn upon his own family's problems since the relationship of the mother and father in the piece has similarities to that which he has described about his own parents in *Man and Child*. Henriette mentions that her husband is lazy, not interested in working, and would prefer to spend his time playing the violin. She notices a violin in "A."'s room, indicating both that "A." could be the son that she is seeking and also signifying Adamov's own concern that he would end up like his father. She observes that her husband gambled away most of his money and that she had to send her son to try to get him away from the casinos. In a situation exactly like that experienced by Adamov as a youngster, the father would tell the boy: "Go tell your mother that I am winning and that I will come home . . . in about half an hour" (*NNRF*, p. 441). When the father eventually commits suicide by throwing himself in front of a train, the boy feels responsible for the act, just as Adamov shared a similar remorse over his own father's suicide. The real-life incident recounted in *Man and Child* originally occurred in 1933 and was now recreated in his theater of 1953, a guilt feeling which the playwright had still not been able to overcome.

In spite of himself, "A." cannot avoid the strength of the mother figure who draws him into her orbit. Like most of the mothers in Adamov's plays, she is strong, shrewd, and overwhelming. In this case, "A." regresses to his childhood, becoming the little boy who lost the ball in the corridor. Whether he is André, the boy being sought, or whether he is another, the effect is the same. He has now become a child and will abandon his marriage, since that would represent a major contact with the real world, a momentous step toward maturity, and, most significantly, a solid relationship with a woman. All of this, Adamov suggests, is what the mother does not want; she prefers to have her youngster back. Claiming that he is dirty, Henriette starts to clean him up. Like the child which he has become, "A." allows himself to be undressed and put to bed. The mother has now achieved what she has been seeking: Everything is *comme nous avons été*. Paralleling the mother in *The Invasion*, Henriette has put matters back in order. However, implies the dramatist, order for the mother means death for the man.

The Reunions was written in 1954 and published in *Théâtre II* in 1955. Adamov was not happy with this work either, but did not eliminate it from his theater. In large measure, this is a continuation of *As We Were*. In the previous play, Adamov shows how the family, particularly the mother, forces the young man to become a child again. In *The Reunions*, "A.", now having become Edgar, tries to break out, to establish his independence, only to find himself caught again in the vise, apparently trapped in a constant reduplication of efforts. Each time that he thinks that he is making his own way, it is only an illusion and he retreats once more into his childhood patterns. Adamov is saying that the psyche of the person can be so formed by the mother that the child can never break loose, can never function as a responsible adult. As a corollary, he feels guilt and remorse: guilt to himself for not having lived his full life and, most especially, remorse for those about him, whom he has involved in his attempt for adulthood and, having failed, has also betrayed. In the earlier play, the guilt feelings were directed toward the father; in this work, they are for the young woman, the fiancée.

In this second presentation of the theme, Edgar, the Adamov figure in the play, is waiting at a train station in Montpellier where he is studying law, to return on a visit to his home town, Quevy, near the Belgian border.[35] While there, he meets two women: Madeleine, the mother figure, the "happiest of women," (cf. *The Disorder*), and Louise, a secretary. He explains to them that both his mother and fiancée in Quevy want him to return there to become an accountant and give up his law studies: "What do they want of me, after all? A man of my age is free to act in his own way, it seems to me (Pause.) Is it my fault if the best law school is located in Montpellier? (Pause.) They claim that the Mediterranean climate leads one to laziness.

What stupidity! It's very simple: Here, I work, and, at Quevy, do you know what I do? I sleep" (*Th.*, II, 74). The sleeping becomes a symbol of the deadening effect of the life that Edgar leads when he is controlled by his mother and fiancée. Once again Adamov plays on the theme of order and disorder, indicating that the women's sense of order intrudes on Edgar's life, creating a disorder in his mind, preventing him from accomplishing anything: "If I go back there, I'll have to wage war from morning to night, to make them admit that I must get my law degree at any cost" (*Th.*, II, 75). While he is talking, it becomes obvious that Madeleine and Louise are also slowly penetrating Edgar's domain and that he will soon be forced to wage another battle to retain his sense of freedom. In his stage directions, Adamov noted that the roles of Madeleine and the mother (who appears later in the play) would be performed by the same actress, suggesting the continual repetition and duplication of the situation.

The lights dim (Adamov's signal in the play of Edgar's loss of liberty and his steady regression to childhood) and we find Edgar living at Madeleine's house. She has taken the place of the mother and Louise has become the fiancée. He is feverishly trying to classify and arrange his papers, so that he can continue his studies. Like Pierre in *The Invasion*, he complains bitterly about Madeleine's interference in his life, her influence and presence preventing him from progressing. In spite of his complaints, Edgar seems neither willing nor able to do anything about the problem. He has fallen into the same pattern of life that he encountered at Quevy with his real mother and fiancée. Adamov is thus emphasizing that, once the psyche has determined life's cycle, the process of change is extremely difficult. While Edgar may wish to assert his own life style, his personality has been so formulated that he cannot do anything about it; he simply does not have the strength.

In a series of striking images, the dramatist demonstrates how Edgar loses what little sense of independence he has and, like "A." in the previous play, falls back into his childhood pattern. Both the mother and fiancée ignore his real strength and use him for their own trivial ends, asking him to become a delivery boy while he is studying so that he can help them out. Louise even brings him her bicycle so that he may use it on his deliveries: The fact that she gives him a girl's bicycle is an indication of her judgment of him as a man, the fact that Edgar cannot ride the bicycle without falling is an obvious

reference to his inability to function sexually. Later, since he is busy
and does not have time to see her, Louise leaves him for a few days
to visit friends. In doing this, she is killed in a train accident. Edgar
now decides to return home to see his real mother and fiancée,
and Madeleine accompanies him on the train. She has brought some
chicken to eat and throws the bones on the floor. Edgar, denoting
his complete, almost canine-like subservience, sits on the floor of
the train, sucking at the bones which she casts off. Finally, upon his
return home, he finds that his fiancée, Lina, has been killed in a
train accident, crushed while riding her bicycle, again an indication
of Edgar's neglect of her as a woman. Completely overcome, the
young man now falls under the total domination of the real mother,
who "pushes him into a baby carriage. Edgar, grotesque, struggles;
his legs stick out of the carriage. The Mother, laughing more and
more heartily, pushes the carriage with her foot, making it career
across the stage from left to right until it disappears into the wings"
(*Th.*, II, 94). Like the *Mutilé* in *The Maneuver*, man has once more
become woman's helpless plaything. Edgar has also lived up to his
own self-fulfilling prophecy: "The perpetual presence of the mother
creates in the child a . . . disastrous weakening. There is nothing
like it to prevent his evolution, to stop him from becoming a man
among men" (*Th.*, II, 85).

As in *As We Were*, Adamov also manifests his own guilt feelings
which, for the first time in his theater, are directly related to human
beings. These feelings are no longer nebulous impressions of blame
leading in no direction. Just as the train was used to show remorse
over the father, it will also take the lives of Louise and Lina. In both
cases, their deaths are caused by Edgar's neglect and essential indifference. They are symbols of Edgar's (and Adamov's) guilt over
not living up to his responsibilities as a mature adult, over his
inability to function as a man (undoubtedly a reference to the playwright's impotence), and, particularly, over his pain at not being
able to communicate as a human being. It is not too surprising that
no guilt feelings at all are displayed toward the mother. In *The
Reunions*, Madeleine and the mother are both described as being
sickly at one point, a reminder, perhaps, of Adamov's own mother
who died of tuberculosis in a hospital. By the end of the play,
however, the mother is pictured as having completely recovered,
suddenly in perfect health, possibly signifying that her influence
will survive even her death.

While both plays contain much that is important in the context of Adamov's total theater, they are too personal and too allusive to be appreciated by any wide audience and therefore must be classified among the playwright's secondary works; yet, the two dramas were of value to the dramatist. As the characters grew more lifelike in their portrayal, and as Adamov realized the extent of his responsibility as well as the role his family played in his neuroses, the weaknesses of the protagonist also became more apparent. In Adamov's first few works, the central figures struggled against an unidentified force that seemed to be so overwhelming in its namelessness that the acceptance of defeat was understandable. But in these two works it seems possible to struggle, for the opponents are also human beings. While the psyche may control man to such an extent that he cannot function properly, once the source of the difficulty is determined, it is less easy to accept the complete passivity and inaction which both characters present. Adamov finally seems to be placing a little of the fault not on the "others," but on the main character. This slow but steady progression toward an awareness of his situation and the ability to do something about it (at least in his writing) seems to have been realized. Adamov saw this as the most significant factor in the play: "*The Reunions* has been very important for me, because, having finished it, reread it and examined it carefully, I understood that it was time to end the exploitation of the semi-dream and of the old family conflict. In a more general way, thanks to *The Reunions*, I think that I have done away with everything which at first allowed me to write and then ended up by preventing me from writing" (*Th.*, II, 15). Adamov realized that he had been utilizing the same approach too long, that his plays, while containing subtle differences, were becoming tiresome and repetitious. He was now able to advance to a different form of theater.

XI *August Strindberg, Dramaturge*
(August Strindberg, Dramatist)

Before he did so, Adamov, with the help of Maurice Gravier,[36] completed a short study on August Strindberg in 1955. Adamov's work was not meant to be comprehensive, but rather was intended as an analysis of Strindberg's writings by means of a close inspection of a few of his plays, emphasizing certain key scenes. This study, written with perception, is a surprisingly rational, scholarly approach to the Swedish dramatist, with extensive citations from his plays.

The most interesting aspect of the work, however, is to be found in the attitudes of Strindberg with which Adamov felt a definite kinship and which were reflected in the French playwright's theater. In discussing Strindberg, Adamov recognized that he, Adamov, was often as much the real subject as the Swedish dramatist: "Moreover, it would have been difficult for me to approach such a question without speaking of myself, for I really believe that it is Strindberg, or more precisely, *The Dream Play*, which prompted me to write for the theater." [37] Adamov had previously admitted to the influence of *The Dream Play* on *The Parody*, but here he indicated that the connection may have been more subtle, less direct. In discussing the influences on Strindberg's theater, he might also be referring to the type of inspiration which he himself had received from the Swedish playwright: "If it is evident that he had numerous [influences], it is nonetheless evident that he found in those from whom he developed . . . more of a confirmation of his own ideas and of his own torments than a new source of inspiration" (*Strindberg*, p. 8).

In Adamov's view, Strindberg's theater is a constant battle, an incessant settling of debts, of people lined up, one against the other. It is also a perpetual vindication of oneself, a constant protest, and, finally, a justification of one's life. The expression "to pay" is the key element in this world of debts and debtors. Such a situation creates a feeling of remorse and hatred at the same time, a statement which also expresses much of Adamov's own sentiments toward those for whom he experienced guilt feelings: "Remorse toward the one whom you have robbed; but hatred for the one to whom you owe something" (*Strindberg*, p. 27).

The Swedish playwright was also conscious of the futility of life, an endless predicament in which everyone is victimized and punished for crimes committed before birth. In order to explain life's mysteries, Strindberg, like Adamov, returned to his childhood and much of his work is autobiographical. In particular, he stressed the theme of the child who is unjustly suspected and punished, as well as that of the child who is guilty but not punished. In one way or another, Strindberg was made to feel guilt and he was driven to seek a scapegoat, hoping to lessen his own feelings of shame, turning his hatred upon his parents, who were the first human beings to humiliate him. Strindberg had an especially strong dislike of his mother and, later, of his wife. His revolt was that of the man before the ungrateful woman and it involved a struggle for power which would be won with the weapons of art and creativity.

Adamov saw Strindberg's theater, like his own, as a theater on the defensive. The Swedish dramatist wanted to prove himself, to justify his actions. Adamov too must have fully understood the use of the stage as an expression of obsessions, since the relationship between neurosis and art was always so strongly a part of his own writing. In both playwrights the literary endeavor was a result of crisis, resulting in the creation on stage of their inner torments. Adamov obviously felt a kinship with the major elements of the Swedish writer's drama: fear, suffering, humiliation, all factors operating as the basis in Adamov's writings. As a result, both men inserted very little real humor into their works, their laughter mainly a mocking expression of life, born of deep bitterness.

Strindberg and Adamov also shared a similar concept of the "others." Like the characters in *The Invasion*, the "others" in Strindberg's theater invade one's life, preventing one from developing. In a definition very much like that of Sartre, Strindberg called hell the permanent ascendancy of one person over another. The "others," then, are the intruders, the imposters, the images of childhood which are still in control.

However, notes Adamov, the real subject of Strindberg's plays is the relationship between dream and reality. The Swedish dramatist approached the theater because he wanted to express a reality that he alone knew, a type of reality caught between the real and the imaginary, between the realm of the half-asleep and the half-awake. Certainly, the author of *Professor Taranne* felt a strong sense of identification here, understanding that the dream world, with its sentiments of doubt, uncertainty, and disorientation, was an important basis of his own theater.

Adamov saw a great deal in Strindberg that added to his own concept of theater and gave him new and fresh insights into his efforts to liberate himself through the stage. Moreover, in one of the more revealing statements in his study, he comments on the poetry which he saw in Strindberg's plays, "born of repetition, or rather of semirepetition, of a parallelism which is not quite one, of a slight variation of original motives. A game of fragile surprises in an edifice of monotony" (*Strindberg*, p. 60). To a great extent, this is the real definition of Adamov's own theater in this first phase of his writing: a theater of subtle, unique variations, yet somewhat tedious repetitions on a similar theme, providing thoughtfully different interpretations of the sorrows of existence.

CHAPTER 3

The Curable Evil

A RTHUR Adamov was now ready to move on to another development in his writing. Having utilized the stage as an expression of his neuroses, he had managed at this point in his life to find a way to cope with his obsessions.[1] Noticing with some satisfaction that the critics had a tendency to join his name with those of Beckett and Ionesco, he at first experienced a certain pleasure. However, he soon added, "I began to judge my first plays severely and, very sincerely, I criticized *Waiting for Godot* and *The Chairs* for the same reasons. I already saw in the 'avant-garde' an easy escape, a diversion from the real problems, the words 'absurd theater' already irritated me. Life was not absurd—only difficult, very difficult" (*HE*, p. 111). The author was thus in the unusual position of repudiating his early works. It must be pointed out, however, that, as was often the case in Adamov's writing, this extreme reaction on his part was not a true reflection of the situation. As his neuroses came under some form of control, he had the opportunity to expand the political and social interests which had always been present since the beginning, although in a lesser way. He was now of the opinion that life contained more than the cruel hand of fate and that man was able to be responsible to himself and to others. This was the curable evil with which he must deal: "The theater must show, simultaneously but well differentiated, both the curable and the incurable aspect of things. The incurable aspect, we all know, is that of the inevitability of death. The curable aspect is the social one."[2]

I *The Perfect Balance:* Le Ping-Pong

In this second phase of his writing, Adamov went to another extreme: In plays such as *Paolo Paoli* and *Le Printemps 71*, he emphasized the political and social realities to such an extent that his theater became almost a diatribe and harangue. However, before he plunged entirely into this second period, in 1954–1955 he composed *Le Ping-Pong*, a transitional work and considered by some critics to be the best play that he ever wrote.[3] At this particular point in his progress as a writer, the dramatist seemed to have controlled his neuroses sufficiently to provide a broader, more concrete, more universal expression to his anguish and torment. At the same time, he had not yet adopted the overwhelmingly Marxist or political orientation which many of his later plays contained. It is precisely because *Ping-Pong* is a transitional work which avoids extremes that the play succeeds so well.

In this work, the futility of human action is presented in counterpoint to the effects on the individual of the capitalist system: "Here the how and the why of human Failure are precisely situated; it is now a matter of the particular failure of two young men who are victims both of their own phantasms and of the temptations offered by a certain society organized with profit as the goal."[4] In twelve tableaux, almost as episodic as a novel, *Ping-Pong* traces the lives of two men from youth to old age, as they dissipate their energies on an obsession for a pinball machine. At the beginning, Arthur is a young art student, Victor is studying to be a doctor.[5] Both men are intrigued by a pinball machine at Madame Duranty's café, and soon their involvement with the machine is so great that it becomes the center of their lives, virtually their only goal. They see it for its various possibilities: as a business venture, for they are aware that Sutter, an employee of the company that owns the machines, comes to collect the coins which are deposited and Victor and Arthur dreamily imagine the profits involved; as a technical challenge, providing them with the opportunity to improve the apparatus; and finally as a poetic endeavor, allowing Arthur to make use of his creative and imaginative talents.

Because of their suggestions they manage to enter the consortium which controls the operation of the machines. There they are introduced to the treachery and deceit of big business, which is interested only in obtaining money. Arthur and, in part, Victor are now dominated by the machine and exist only in their connection to it. Their human contacts are also based upon this same obsession: Each of the characters in the play revolves around the apparatus and the resultant love, friendship, fear, and hatred of daily living develop as a consequence of the characters' interrelationships with each other and with the machine. In so doing, they destroy their lives through a wasteful commitment, betraying their more genuine and honest human values. As all of the characters grow older and

it becomes evident that their associations with the pinball machine
have ruined them, Victor and Arthur are seen in the final, compelling
tableau, this time playing table tennis, a new obsession as absurd
and foolish as their previous preoccupation. Even at this point, each
man continues to change the rules and perfect the game to such an
extent that the whole project becomes a farce. Victor collapses and
dies, leaving Arthur alone.

Adamov's first inspiration for the play was the image of two
old men playing table tennis. He did not know what the subject
of his work would be, but he knew how he would end it, having
the perfect opportunity to show that all human action results in
the same wastefulness, eventually leading to death. Once he had
the overall image in mind, the playwright then took a specific
incident from his own life: "The first concrete idea of *Ping-Pong*
came at the Mabillon [a café in the Saint-Germain des Prés
section in Paris], while playing a pinball machine named 'The
Rocket and the Moon.' The player was supposed to operate it
in such a way that the rocket reached the moon. The machine
then lighted up, the game was won" (*HE*, p. 112). From this pastime
in his personal life, Adamov saw how his work could be enlarged,
preferring to use the pinball machine as the main image of his
play, rather than the game of table tennis, because of the former's
closer links to the business world and the capitalist system. The
theme of this play was very personal to Adamov, who had seen his
father fritter away and destroy his life because of his exaggerated
preoccupation with gambling, an exercise in futility similar to that
experienced by Victor and Arthur.

Once he began the writing, Adamov made the pinball machine
the center around which everything turned, like Lili in *The Parody*:
"*Ping-Pong*, with its purposely deceptive title, has the pinball
machine as its real subject. I wanted the play to revolve around
the obsession for this pinball machine. I wanted it to be the center
of all the concerns, yearnings, ambitions" (*HE*, p. 112). In a sense,
the pinball apparatus replaces the fatality of the former plays.
As a result, the characters have greater freedom, or as Adamov
termed it, "indecision," than in previous works. In spite of the
givens of the situation in which each one will inevitably fail, they
do have a certain independence. They are fighting a machine,
a part of the capitalist system, not simply the destiny that awaits
all men. This time the enemy is not the uncontrollable disturbance

of the psyche brought about by the fatality of life. Arthur and Victor can avoid what is happening to them: "Contrary to what takes place in my other plays . . . the threat does not come only from outside; the characters secrete their own poison, prepare their own unhappiness; and this unhappiness, not having exactly the same cause for each one, does not have the same results" (*Th.*, II, 16–17). In *Combat*, Adamov commented on the greater degree of complexity and individualization of his characters: "My machine is not a symbol. Rather, it is a center of interest for each one, according to his age, character, or social position. For some, it is an object that they want to keep, to protect. For others, it is an instrument of domination. For Sutter, the possibility of impressing the world. For Arthur, an escape from this world, a trapeze for the acrobatics of his brain. For Victor, a simple pastime."[6]

In fact, each of the characters is defined or distinguished by his relation to and utilization of the machine. Annette, who is the principal female figure, sees the instrument as an opportunity to achieve a better position in life. To that end, she uses the men around her who can help her gain entrance to the consortium. In spite of her goal, she often seems to share Arthur's enthusiasm for the creative possibilities of the machine, and Adamov endows her with more sympathy than he normally does his women characters. For Madame Duranty, the mother figure, the apparatus is only an overt indication of how life has treated her badly. When it breaks down, she loses money. Existence becomes a perpetual complaint because of her inability to get the machine repaired and to put her affairs back in order. In this context, Madame Duranty is basically the same as the whining mother figures of the previous plays.

Those who work at the consortium reflect Adamov's contemptuous view of the world of big business. Sutter and Roger are both employed by the company, but neither one has any real interest in the pinball operation; their work is simply a means to an end, a way to power, fame, and money. But it is the director of the consortium, *Le Vieux* (The Old Man), for whom Adamov reserves his greatest scorn. Seeing the whole operation not only as a money-making proposition, but as a close link to sexual conquests, *Le Vieux* manipulates people for his own purposes. He asks Annette to become a spy for his group, promises Madame Duranty that he will fix her machine if she will sign a petition for him, accepts Arthur's and Victor's ideas, planning to use them and to keep the credit to himself. In short, the playwright suggests that *Le Vieux* represents the capitalist system, exploiting others for its own profitable goals. The Old Man is willing to sacrifice quality for quantity in his frenzied desire for money. At the same time, he is willing to sacrifice people in his quest for power, a prefiguration of the characters in *Paolo Paoli*.

The two principal figures, who were inspired in part by Flaubert's *Bouvard et Pécuchet*,[7] are also presented in their interreaction with the pinball machine. Victor, in a lesser way, shares many of the same business ideals of *Le Vieux*. He views the enterprise as a moneymaking proposition and participates in it to the extent that it can prove useful to him. Other than that, his interest is superficial and passing and yet even he cannot avoid an obsessive involvement. The more practical of the two men, he has gone on to become a doctor. Nevertheless, in spite of his detachment, he is unable to separate himself from the machine's influence, finding that he can obtain his patients by going to the places where people play the game.

On the other hand, Arthur, presumably Adamov himself, is the poet, the visionary. Of all of the characters, Arthur is the most truly interested in the pinball machine for its creative possibilities. Although, like Victor, he may appreciate its moneymaking aspects, he can also relish the infinite variations which the instrument has to provide, with the reduction of its side flippers, the addition of the extra ball, the rocket reaching the moon. For him, the game becomes such an obsession that it dominates his life. In his own way, Arthur uses this preoccupation as a means of escape from the world surrounding him. He becomes the very image of man's alienation, virtually deifying a machine, while distorting his human relationships. Even his friendship with Victor suffers when the latter becomes less interested in the game.

Arthur becomes the exaggeration of those who are entrapped in the orbit of the machine, his situation only a magnification of what is happening to the other characters. Since he has given each character a certain degree of differentiation, Adamov reveals an even more pronounced pessimism about life. In the previous works, there was nothing that man *could* do. In this play, there is nothing that man *will* do. Each character fails to cope with reality, continually striving to reach his own paradise via the machine, allowing the capitalist system to use him. Each personage could manipulate his destiny in a limited way, but does not; each one is at least partially responsible for what happens to him. Sutter becomes a virtual beggar, Roger disappears, Madame Duranty is reduced to poverty and senile complaining, *Le Vieux* dies—a victim of his own emotions, Annette is killed by a taxi, either a suicide or an accident victim, Victor dies while foolishly pursuing his game of table tennis, and Arthur remains alone after having devoted his life to a wasteful and destructive goal, a life now empty and hollow.[8]

Yet in spite of their individualization and greater complexity, the characters in the play are not meant to exist as psychologically-developed beings, as they would in the naturalistic theater. They do not possess a soul, and are identified mainly through their connection with the machine. Since the situations in which they find themselves are spurious, their language must also be false: Their words are clichés, stereotypes, and truisms, they sound as if they are reciting something which they have memorized, something lifeless. Roland Barthes, calling the play a series of *situations de langage*, comments: "*Ping-Pong* is entirely constituted by a block of language under glass, analogous, if you wish, to those frozen vegetables which allow the English to enjoy the tartness of spring in their winter."[9] Since man has not really accepted the freedom of his responsibility, his language is not free. Language is thus an indication of his refusal to face reality: There is no sense of spontaneity, everything is thought out before it is spoken. Because the speeches do not allow for deviation from the set pattern which has been learned, there can be no communication.

The language represents the position in which the characters find themselves. Placed in situations which are clearly wasteful—situations in which they use enormous amounts of energy, time, and thought on the refinement of a game which is mere child's play—the characters are required to use a speech pattern which carries the same distortion, becoming a parody of their actions. As Martin Esslin points out, in an interesting comment on the use of language in the work, "This is a play that may well appear completely meaningless if it is merely read. The speeches about improvements in the construction of pinball machines may seem trivial nonsense; the meaning of the play emerges precisely at the moment that the actor delivers these nonsensical lines with a depth of conviction worthy of the loftiest flights of poetry. It is a play that has to be acted *against* the text rather than with it." [10] The mission of the characters is inane, but they engage in it seriously and persistently, revealing the absurdity of their world. In *The Invasion*, Adamov had utilized indirect language in cases where the characters did not express their real opinions but hid their feelings behind idle conversation, a technique used by Chekhov. But in *Ping-Pong*, the characters proclaim their foolish notions with religious intensity: "In Chekhov, real feelings are suppressed behind meaningless politeness, in *Le Ping-Pong* absurd ideas are proclaimed as if they were eternal truths." [11] In Adamov's work, language is one of the signs of man's sense of estrangement—mankind is doomed to failure because there is no point of human contact.

Yet, the weakness of the individual human being is not the only cause of the isolation which we all suffer. Adamov now suggests more strongly than in previous works that the *strength* of other human beings working toward their own perverted goals creates the capitalist system, which must also share a great deal of the blame: "Alienation . . . of man captive in a society in which the pinball machine sparkles, rules, sits in state. It [the pinball machine] does not yet clearly specify the society of which it is the image, but my half-willed, half-involuntary imprecision does not prevent one from recognizing the guilty party: the capitalist system" (*HE*, p. 112). Unlike the procedure in his later plays, Adamov does not place the blame entirely on the world of big business but, for the first time, he does make it one of the specific enemies in man's struggle. The director of the consortium typifies the system's craftiness and willful disregard for people, its exploitation of others. Adamov wants to stress that all those involved in the system lack any real interest in the project for itself: They want only the power and money which can be derived from it. Thus the basis for all the activity springs from a society that is false and a goal founded on twisted premises.

Rather than a frontal assault on the capitalist system, however, *Ping-Pong* shows that when man allows himself to be controlled by any idea or ideology, he loses his freedom and becomes a slave to the organization which develops around it. The pinball machine is the image of man's objective—a silly, childish game. But for all those involved in the project, it is a serious question of their existence, eventually even a matter of life and death. Because of their obsession with the machine, an entire network of interrelationships and structures has developed, involving, implies Adamov, those who exploit and those who are exploited. By giving their lives over to a machine, by hoping that it will give them power and love, Victor, Arthur, and the others have let themselves be manipulated. This foolish project, very much a part of the capitalist world, has become the real enslaver. At this particular moment in his writing, the playwright had not yet placed the full responsibility on the capitalist system. Victor and Arthur can still pull themselves out of the quicksand into which they are sinking. Yet, like the playwright's father, they cannot help what they do and the system draws them in even more deeply. While each character is provided with some "indecision," it is clear that he cannot liberate himself entirely from his obsessions, he cannot face the world as it really is. Adamov's theater is still one of general human considerations; in spite of the dramatist's turn toward the outer world, he has not yet left the realm of the inner being.

It is precisely because he remained too much in this realm that Adamov later criticized the play. He felt that he had not sufficiently developed the workings of the consortium and that he had left that aspect too detached from the piece as a whole. Although he recognized that he had made an ever greater step toward reality by placing the action in a fixed time and place, he nevertheless noted that "the social events which, in the course of the years, change the internal organization of the consortium, are not truly indicated, so that one does not really feel the state of society on the one hand and the passage of time on the other. . . . I should have tried to examine the wheels of the great social machine as carefully and as minutely as I had examined the bumpers and side flippers of the pinball machine. This is the examination I am trying to undertake today in a new play, situated even more firmly in a time and place than *Ping-Pong*" (*Th.*, II, 17).[12]

In spite of the playwright's disclaimer, *Ping-Pong* is one of Adamov's best works and he has been unfair in his judgment. Although he is still depicting the same theme, we are now confronted with the how and the why of life's situations, to use Madame Serreau's terms. The effect of the analysis allows us to understand the workings behind the feelings; the theme is no longer so closely allied with the dramatist's own psyche that, as in many of his earlier plays, the spectator cannot appreciate it. Now we can comprehend the efforts behind man's foolish actions. The image of the pinball apparatus is surely one of the most striking in his theater: The ridiculous aberrations of the characters around the machine become the visual representation of the truly tragic meaning of life's wastefulness.

In the final analysis, it was a wise decision on Adamov's part not to emphasize the workings of the consortium. As the play stands, it contains the right combination of the inner and outer worlds, the psyche and reality. Although it is true that the world which he has created deals only with the preoccupations of the characters and has little in common with the normal routine of living, this is not a weakness—it is rather an effective structural device that reflects the narrow vision of the people involved. What we see in *Ping-Pong* reveals the very limited arena in which Victor and Arthur operate. If Adamov had stressed the economic and social situation, he would have destroyed the very delicate balance which he had created. Having made his own terror more specific, but having not yet introduced the strongly Marxist overtones of his following works, the playwright succeeded in finding an excellent blend of the personal and historical elements which would henceforth constitute the basis of his theater. In addition, *Ping-Pong*, along with *Professor Taranne*, is one of the two works by the playwright which seem to be faithful to the spirit in which they were composed. All of his other plays, including those which follow *Ping-Pong*, reveal an exaggerated involvement on the dramatist's part which becomes almost as neurotic and obsessed as the principal characters in the plays.

Ping-Pong has remained one of Adamov's more popular dramas. It was first presented in Paris at the Théâtre des Noctambules on March 2, 1955, under the direction of Jacques Mauclair, who comments: "The creation of *Ping-Pong* constituted an important step in Adamov's career and in his relationship with the public. He came out of the ghetto of the authors of the damned, condemned to clandestine theaters. Adamov no longer, understandably, wanted to hear one speak of the 'Tuesdays at the *Oeuvre*' or of performances given at 6 o'clock stealthily before three spectators. Performed at the Noctambules at 9 P.M., he was well received by the press and the play had, if I remember correctly, more than 150 performances, which was an unhoped-for number."[13]

In this transitional work, Adamov created one of his most accessible plays, one which has been performed numerous times around the world, including productions in New York, London, West Berlin, and Stockholm. At this point in his career, the dramatist was concerned with both the incurable and the curable elements in life. However, as he continued to write over the next few years, he would turn particularly to the social or curable elements for his subject matter.

II   *The Expressionists, Brecht, and Marx*

In effecting this change, Adamov did not abandon entirely his first style of writing, but simply emphasized different elements which had always been present. Certainly he did not discard the technical innovations which connected him with the avant-garde theater, as his later plays would testify; nor did Artaud's work fail to continue to influence him throughout his career. Like his mentor, Adamov continued to use the stage as an arena for a physical expression of ideas, a place in which the dialogue competed with lighting, sets, and mime in the total performance. However, having completed ten plays, the dramatist did feel confident enough in himself and in his writing to eliminate the strong dependence upon the dreamlike play which Strindberg had inspired. More important, he no longer had to justify himself through his theater. In this second phase, the world of paranoid obsessions and fantasy, while still a part of the whole, was considerably reduced in significance.

One of the influences which helped pave the way for Adamov's transition from the vague, highly personal dramas to the ideological plays of his second period may have been the German Expressionist drama. The German-speaking Adamov was acquainted with the theater of this country—in 1953, he had translated Büchner's *Danton's Death* and was particularly impressed with the same author's *Woyzeck*.[14] The Expressionists, who appeared around 1900 and flourished into the twenties, rebelled against authority and convention in art as well as in life; they refused to accept the "realistic" theater and the idea of a "well-made play." Their spiritual allies were the Surrealists, with whom Adamov had had contacts, and they were also inspired by Strindberg and his "dream" plays.

In their dramas, they made use of extremism and distortion, with disjointed, loose plots, characters who spoke past rather than to each other, language which became almost telegraphic in its wording—all aspects which anticipated the alienating effects of the drama of the absurd and which Adamov incorporated into his own theater. In the Expressionist plays, as in Strindberg's dream works, the "projection and embodiment of psychic forces take the place of imitation of external facts; association of ideas supplants construction of plot based on logical connection of cause and effect. The old structural principle of causal interrelation between character, incident, and action gives way to a new structural pattern, closer to music than to drama—the presentation and variation of a theme." [15] In this type of theater, psychic situations were projected onto the stage, the invisible part of the subconscious was visualized, and the psychological problems of the mind were made over into a vivid, concrete happening. In such an approach, language became less important, and experiments were undertaken to diversify its uses, like repetition or contrapuntal dialogue, experiments also used by Adamov in his theater. Sometimes in Expressionist works, silences or pauses became an integral part of the action in the attempt to relate a type of truth which conventional theater could not capture.

Instead of a carefully-knit plot, the Expressionist drama generally included a series of episodic situations in which the emphasis was placed upon "show" or demonstration of themes rather than upon action or plot. As such, it approached a pageant-type framework in which the theme was expressed by means of a loosely-connected story with a series of "stations" or situations. In part at least, the Expressionist writers were intent upon drawing a picture of a meaningless, wildly materialistic world in terms which often approached caricature and the realm of the absurd. In addition, they were interested in life in all its many ramifications: "They constituted not merely an aesthetic, but also an ethical, social, and sometimes even political revolt." [16] Expressionism was closely allied with pacifism, humanitarianism, and socialism, and it is probable that this concern for man as a social and political being helped provide Adamov with another model as he turned to a new development in his writing. In his next works, Adamov would use the various techniques of the Expressionists as he began to comment on the political and social conditions of the world around him.

At the same time, the German playwright, Bertolt Brecht, along with the director Erwin Piscator, would also play a major, perhaps even greater, role in Adamov's orientation. The French public and press became aware of the new Brecht drama, with its innovative techniques and principles when, in 1954, Brecht's *Berliner Ensemble* came to Paris for the first time as part of the International Theater Festival held in that city. Adamov and Roger Planchon, who was to direct Adamov's next play, attended many of the presentations of the company. Little by little, as he became favorably impressed with Brecht and his vision, the dramatist's views on the validity of purely avant-garde theater began to change.

Not surprisingly, the Brechtian theater had some relationship to the Expressionist movement, as both groups wanted to demonstrate or prove a point. The difference between the two was that the Expressionists generally wanted to appeal to the emotions, while the "epic" theater addressed itself to the critical intelligence of the spectator.[17] The German playwright, along with Piscator and his political theater, aimed at turning the stage into a place for the presentation of and the reflection upon current problems and ideas. This would be achieved, in Brecht's theory, by forcing the audience to think about matters that have occurred at a given time and place in the past; in this "epic" or historical theater, the audience must be constantly reminded that it is merely getting an accounting of something that has already taken place. It is the theater's task to destroy any idea that a real action is happening on stage. The German dramatist further wanted to discourage any sort of identification with the characters in the play,[18] leading to the diffusion of the famous term, *Verfremdungseffekt*, a situation in which the audience is kept separated or alienated from the action. In this type of drama, no attempt is made to create highly individualized characterizations. Rather, the characters come out of the social function of the individual and change with that function. Like the Expressionist plays, Brecht's "epic" work is episodic, generally revolving around particular scenes which can almost exist entirely by themselves like chapters in a novel. In addition, the nonliterary elements of the production have their own independence and autonomy, rivaling or surpassing that assigned to the text, all with the view of breaking down any form of illusion.

It is thus understandable that Adamov should have taken such a strong liking to Brecht's work, which he considered the most important in the twentieth century. In large measure, the German dramatist was simply an extension of the many ideas that Adamov had already found so suitable in Artaud, the Expressionists, and, to some degree, in Strindberg. However, Brecht offered an important basis for future Adamovian plays: a theater founded on historical, economic, and social considerations. As Adamov grew less involved with his personal problems, the Brechtian model furnished a significant motivation for his writing.

Outside events also played a major part. During the composition of both *Ping-Pong* and the next play, *Paolo Paoli*, various incidents on the international scene brought the political realm much more strongly to Adamov's consciousness. Stalin died in 1953 and the massive block of the Soviet Union began to change, allowing Adamov to accept communism more readily. In addition, the former French colonies of Morocco and Tunisia became independent in the middle 1950's, while in November, 1954, the Algerian war began, with Adamov taking a strong position against the colonists. In October, 1956, the Soviets crushed the rioting in Hungary. Adamov commented in his journal: "Most people do not seem to notice that the very day that the events of Hungary took place, the English and the French landed at the Suez Canal. Certainly a curious coincidence. Anticommunism is unleashed" (*HE*, p. 120).

These events, along with Brecht's theater, were influential in leading Adamov along his new direction, a course which had already been suggested in works like *One Against Another* and *The Direction of the March*. The dramatist was not only searching for a more realistic theater, but he now intended to link this realism to a Marxist viewpoint. In that respect Brecht's theory of alienation proved most appropriate. Hans Egon Holthusen's observations on the German playwright also provide some insight into the Brecht–Marxist influence on Adamov's writing:

It is not an accident that "alienation" (*Verfremdung*) reminds us so conspicuously of the concept "estrangement" (*Entfremdung*) created by Hegel and borrowed by Marx. Estrangement primarily and taken quite generally means the disharmony which always reappears between the world as it has come to be and the pressing forces of historical progress. Then, however, in its specifically Marxist interpretation, it comes to mean the state of progressive deterioration and oppression into which the human being must fall when he has no share of the means of production controlled by the capitalist system, sees himself degraded to a commodity and no longer disposes over himself and his life. Alienation is thus no more than a portrayal of estrangement, i.e., making estrangement "striking." There is no doubt about its final goal: it is the removal of estrangement—it is revolution.[19]

Adamov's theater was also to take on a Marxist overtone. The characters had not only emerged from "no-man's-land" but were now going to be defined in relation to previously indefinable external circumstances. At this juncture, the playwright agreed with Brecht that the "epic" theater "alone could present the complexity of the human condition in an age in which the life of individuals could no longer be understood in isolation from the powerful trend of social, economical and historical forces affecting the lives of millions."[20] Like Karl Marx, the other influence in his new commitment, Adamov felt that the economic substructure was what gave form and character to the social, political, and ideological superstructure of society at every stage of human history. The basis of Marx's theory was the idea of the labor theory of value, in which man, part of the labor force, became a commodity: "It is primarily a price theory, according to which 'commodities' should exchange on the basis of the 'socially necessary' labor time devoted to their production."[21] In this view, which would play an important role in Adamov's future theater, man would become a product whose labor value could be exchanged. This dehumanization of man, as well as a deepening misery caused by intolerable conditions would, according to Marx, lead to a socialist revolution in which the future society and economy would fully utilize man's talents for the satisfaction of human needs. Such ideas became a significant part of Adamov's second phase.

In an article published in 1956, while he was in the process of writing *Paolo Paoli*, Adamov revealed the new direction of his theater, stating both explicitly and implicitly his debt to the theories of Brecht and Marx.[22] He now felt that it was possible to envisage the idea of an historical drama, placed in a specific period (usually twenty years from the present, not too far away to make a legend out of it and not too up-to-date so that it touched upon a current reality), in which there would be no identification with the characters. Rather, there would be a critical awareness of the times in which one was living and this awareness would be related to the people and the incidents presented on stage.[23] In other words, the play was to provide the spectator with the opportunity to judge his moment in history through an intellectual consideration of the action on stage. In the presentation, Adamov continued, the main subject would be the coexistence and the antagonism of the classes in which one group was always oppressed by the other, or others. At this point in his writing, Adamov claimed that it was especially important that this state of oppression never be considered as a result of the unchangeable aspect of human nature or as the result of an inevitable destiny. The theater must be *démystifiant* (demystifying), it must show the audience how the machine behind the operations works: "It is always profitable from a social point of view, and fertile from a theatrical point of view, to disclose the ruses by means of which those in power try to divide those organizations which are dangerous to them."[24] To present this spectacle of disharmony, of the grotesque disproportion between the false outer spectacle and the real misery of mankind, Adamov felt that Brecht was the best equipped in the theatrical world.

Adamov's drama was now going to reveal the "real" tragedy of man's exploitation of his fellowman; his new theater would point out that history is made by men, living beings capable of change. The implacable, relentless hand of destiny would no longer be dominant. This did not mean, he added, that he would completely eliminate what amounted to a true use of fate in his theater ("the incurable evil—sickness which comes from some unknown place, misfortunes which strike one for some irrational reason"), for it cannot be denied that fate does play a strong role in man's life. He would rather, however, emphasize the force and strength of the human will, an equally important factor in man's existence.

III   *History and Political Commitment:* Paolo Paoli

Paolo Paoli is the first play written in Adamov's "new" style. Perhaps his favorite work (in *Man and Child*, he devotes an entire chapter to it), this is his first attempt to take a specific, factual subject, placing it in an historical context. The play represents an abandonment of some of the philosophical principles of Adamov's first phase of writing and an acceptance of an ideological, political commitment; life's incurable element is only one part of the total picture. The dramatist now emphasizes the curable aspects, studying the workings of society, analyzing its defects, and suggesting improvements.

An ambitious play, with a rich, complex, sometimes confusing mingling of social, economic, and historical background, *Paolo Paoli* deals with the circulation of merchandise in the capitalist system in France and its overseas territories during the *belle époque*, the "banquet years," from 1900–1914. Ostensibly, the merchandise for sale is the comically absurd selection of butterflies and ostrich feathers. In actual fact, Adamov wants the audience to see that the real product being manipulated is man, who is exploited and utilized by his fellowmen in their quest for financial gain. The playwright links the fate of the individual to the times and background of which he is a part: "*Paolo Paoli* is, in fact, situated very precisely in this period [1900–1914], and the evolution of the characters is conditioned by the unfolding of the events of the world in which they live."[25] No longer is his theater placed in an indefinite period with characters detached from the world around them; the theater is to be the realm of the specific. For the first time, Adamov will attempt a political and social satire of the twentieth century.

The dramatist came upon the subject of his play by accident. In order to make a living, since his theater could not provide him with a substantial enough income, he had taken on a number of writing chores, especially translations into French of works like Georg Büchner's *Danton's Death*, Heinrich von Kleist's *The Broken Pitcher*, and Strindberg's *The Pelican*. In the Spring of 1955, with the aid of his wife, he agreed to "rewrite" the memoirs of Eugène Le Moult, an entomologist who had made his fortune by utilizing the convicts in Cayenne[26] to find butterflies for his business: "Le Moult is a scoundrel, but it does not matter since, by listening to him evoke his past, the idea came to me for my play, *Paolo Paoli*" (*HE*, p. 117). Adamov was immediately attracted to both the comic and tragic elements of the portrait of the convict chasing after butterflies with his net. He realized that this picturesque image was only a diversion from the real, bitter truth: The butterfly for the entomologist was not an *objet d'art*, but an object of business; the convict was not an amusing figure but a horrifying example of exploitation. Since these events took place in 1900–1914, Adamov had found the period for his play. He next decided that the entomologist should have a business associate to whom he would sell his products and, after some research, he found the proper complement: a merchant in the feather industry, which, until 1912, was the fourth largest French export trade. Upon further study into the period, he became interested in the separation of church and state and the idea of a priest as a major character came to his mind. He was further helped in the development of his play by reading that certain missionaries in China had also ventured into the butterfly industry, using schoolchildren to seek out the insects for them. The idea of the priest became even clearer when he happened to come upon a brochure in the National Library in Paris written by an abbot in the 1900's. This abbot strongly defended the feather industry, arguing that it was not a crime to kill birds, otherwise why would God have permitted them to fly in the sky? In any case, reported Adamov, the priest felt that it was not such a terrible fate to end up on a lady's hat (*HE*, p. 118).

With these images in mind, the dramatist set about creating a play which would say something about the "curable" situation of man, in which men would be seen in direct relation to the world around them. Dealing with an apparently frivolous topic, the playwright wanted to show the truly tragic dimensions of the human condition. And this was another reason that he chose the "banquet years," for the silliness of the prewar years collided with the reality of World War I: "And if I chose the period before 1914, it is because it was a period which went from the most obvious frivolity to the most dramatic events. So much so that the movement of private life, under the circumstances, could be linked particularly well to that of public life."[27]

In essence, Adamov attempted to provide an accounting of the system of exchange which society had established. The play is so structured that it is the economic mechanism of exchange which determines the movement of the work rather than individual persons. The characters are caught in a network of socioeconomic requirements, trapped in an endless pattern of bargaining and merchandising: They begin by exchanging butterflies and end up by exchanging men. These individuals are, first, a microcosm of society and, then, of nations, struggling and competing for markets, eventually leading to a class fight and finally to World War I. Adamov particularly wanted to stress the circular aspect of such a situation, showing that societies (or the individuals in the societies) allow themselves to be caught in a constant repetition of events which he called *tourbillons circulaires* (circular whirlwinds). In this same context, the dramatist also hoped that the audience would grasp the parallels to be drawn with modern France, which was repeating the same mistakes and committing the same ignominies.[28]

The most remarkable achievement of Adamov's ambitious undertaking is that he managed to portray the religious, political, social, and national complexities of this society by means of only seven characters: Paolo Paoli, a collector and dealer of rare butterflies; Florent Hulot-Vasseur, also a collector of butterflies and an importer and manufacturer of ostrich feathers; the Abbé Saulnier, cunning and devious, a willing accomplice in all the business ventures; Madame de Saint-Sauveur, a captain's wife, the chauvinist, blind to everything but the jingoistic militarism of France; Stella, Paolo's German-born wife, who becomes Hulot-Vasseur's mistress; and finally, the victims, Robert Marpeaux, the convict utilized by Paolo and Hulot-Vasseur for their own commercial purposes, the "commodity," and his wife, Rose, another martyr of exploitation.

Curiously, in spite of Adamov's new approach to theater, the structure of the play is quite similar to that of his previous works. At first *Paolo Paoli* seems like a simple repetition of the construction of *Ping-Pong*. The butterflies and ostrich feathers around which all the characters gravitate and which have become their obsessions are used exactly like the pinball machine of the previous play. In both works, the ridiculousness and absurdity of man's actions are underscored. In addition, the theme of human beings trapped in a web from which they cannot escape had served as the basis of all of his earlier "dream" works, and, once again, two of the major characters—Paolo and Hulot-Vasseur—appear to be heading toward a similar fate.

This time, however, there are some significant differences in the content. While man is still the helpless pawn in the struggles of existence, he is no longer controlled principally by his obsession or by fate: There is a new, "curable" element. The capitalist system and man himself must bear the burden of responsibility. The system is composed of human beings and they must accept the blame for the situation of their fellowmen. At the same time, implies Adamov, man can change this situation through his will, his desires, and his awareness. Although Paolo and Hulot-Vasseur share similar experiences, they are really designed to represent two poles of the economic system, the two ends necessary for the trading and exchanging. Their structural use is no longer meant to convey the essential sameness of man's fate, but the polarity which is the basis of business. Nor do they share the same final role: Paolo rebels against the system and everything represented by Hulot-Vasseur.

Paolo,[29] based on Eugène Le Moult, the original inspiration of the work, is a dealer in butterflies. His father, like Le Moult's, was a minor Corsican civil servant at Cayenne. Recognizing the opportunities for financial gain at the expense of others, Paolo organizes the convicts in the city to work as poorly-paid butterfly hunters for his business in France. One of the young convicts, Marpeaux, serving a sentence for a minor crime, escapes to Venezuela, where he is completely dependent upon Paolo for his livelihood and he must continue to hunt butterflies. Paolo is encouraged in his business ventures by Hulot-Vasseur, the other part of the organization, for Hulot-Vasseur purchases the butterflies for his own commercial undertakings. A shrewd and ruthless industrialist, he is beset with many problems, brought about by the labor conflicts in his factory and his struggle with German competitors. The third member of this unholy trio, Abbé Saulnier, is drawn most willingly into the web of business: His brother is a missionary in China, and when the market becomes difficult for Paolo in that country, the abbot offers his brother's services in obtaining some rare butterfly specimens for Paolo. In the first few scenes, Adamov thus effectively conveys the cruel absurdities as well as the interrelationships of the economic, religious, and penal systems, all against the background of historical events.

In his portrait of Paolo, Hulot-Vasseur, and the priest, Adamov is especially interested in presenting the conniving and treacherousness which he considers a part of the capitalist system. Paolo is a foolish, small-time businessman, making his fortune by selling objects made from butterfly wings—religious pictures, ashtrays, saucers, trays. Hulot-Vasseur exists only for the money and power which he holds, coldly indifferent to human beings as individuals; Paolo, the abbot, and Marpeaux are only pieces to be used in Hulot-Vasseur's overall pursuit of financial success. The priest loses all of his religious trappings and turns into a businessman, becoming probably the most unpleasant character in the play—hypocritical and devious. What is particularly striking about Adamov's picture of Abbé Saulnier is that the priest has no concept of morality or decency. At the very moment that he is approaching Hulot-Vasseur to ask him to aid Marpeaux (a project which his later actions show that he cares nothing about), it develops that he is really asking the industrialist to buy some butterfly specimens from his brother in China, thereby betraying Paolo, to whom he had previously promised the specimens.[30]

The playwright is underlining his point that only the strongest, the most ruthless, the most deceitful can survive in the jungle of the economic system. As the play progresses, Paolo loses most of his business because he is basically a somewhat anarchical, second-rate entrepreneur whose interests clash with the much more concerted and ambitious efforts of major industry. It is Adamov's view that those who are victorious succeed because they know how to make alliances at the right moment, alliances which oftentimes create strange bedfellows: "Finally, what I especially had to show . . was the monstrous alliance, constantly renewed, of the so-called Christians and the so-called anticlericals." [31] Hulot-Vasseur, a militant anticlerical, joins forces with the abbot when it becomes economically profitable for him to do so. Both sides unite to fight against the one whom Adamov sees as the victim in the affair, the worker Marpeaux. Essentially, adds the playwright, it is the worker who is the major threat to the capitalists and their system and they will bury any personal differences in this class struggle in order to keep him subjugated.

Marpeaux, the pawn in the system, has returned from Venezuela to seek pardon from the government. Since the pardon may be some time in coming, Paolo sends him to Morocco in the interval, completely indifferent to the fact that the country has become dangerous because the French are still waging a battle against the natives. It is obvious that Marpeaux is an object to be used, a commodity to be exploited. Upon his return from Morocco, after having obtained his pardon, he joins the Socialist party and opposes the *jaunes*, a militant Catholic organization run by Abbé Saulnier. Working in Hulot-Vasseur's factory, Marpeaux distributes pacifist pamphlets urging soldiers to desert. The abbot, Marpeaux's former protector as long as he was not a threat to the priest's interests, denounces him for subverting the troops and Marpeaux is then arrested. As soon as Paolo hears of this, he has a sudden change of heart and vows that he will no longer help the system, his money will be used for those who really need it: "Mark it well, my friend Saulnier, you can say good-bye to that money. That money will no longer be a part of your dirty little circuit. . . . It will go directly to those who need it to eat, clothe themselves, and to annoy you, which comes to the same thing" (*Th.*, III, 141).

This is the first play in which Adamov has created a "positive" major character (Marpeaux) and a "noble" action (Paolo's attempt to take money out of the capitalist system and turn it over to the needy.[32] Interestingly, both of these aspects are the weakest points in the play. Marpeaux's characterization is not successful because of the one-sidedness of the portrait, the lack of complexity in his makeup. He is so totally "good" that he is less than believable. Although Adamov intended that Marpeaux represent an ideological point of view—the worker struggling against the system—and the author did not want the spectator to identify with the character, it is clear that his own sympathies lay very strongly with Marpeaux. As a result, Adamov has developed a characterization in spite of himself and, unfortunately, a characterization lacking in dimension.

A more serious criticism can be made of the abrupt and unconvincing change of attitude expressed by Paolo at the end. This admirable gesture, found very rarely in Adamov's theater, is utterly unbelievable, especially in view of Paolo's generally negative portrait throughout the rest of the work. It is also hardly likely that Paolo's action will take the money out of circulation as he claims. In any event, he has nothing to lose by his action. It is principally an act of anger against Hulot-Vasseur and Abbé Saulnier who have deserted him now that his business has been ruined by the war. Yet Paolo's gesture is important to the theme of the play because it allows Adamov to show that human beings can do something, that their situations are "curable." By their will power and by their determination, suggests the playwright, they can triumph over the workings of the capitalist system. This is Adamov's call for a limited revolt, based upon human strength and represents the dramatist's hopes for mankind.

It is probable that the author intended to use this final scene as a vivid contrast to the rest of the play. In this last part, Paolo is meant to depict man at his best, working for the betterment of all. For the first time, his words and his deeds coincide. Earlier Paolo and the others of the capitalist system mouthed false, hypocritical words to cover up what they were really doing, the playwright stressing the opposition between "what the characters do and what they say." It is the dramatist's contention that people like Paolo, Hulot-Vasseur, and the abbot speak of "eternal" values but have only temporal interests in mind—their own commercial gains. In this comedy of disproportion, the spectator is meant to recognize the situation of men relentlessly pursuing their business interests, to laugh at the absurdity of their endeavor, and, finally, to realize that this is more than just grotesque foolishness. It is a tragic representation of man's hypocrisy and his exploitation of others. The spectator is to understand that, in this type of system, those who succeed do so at the expense of others. The audience is then expected to take its observations one step further, associating the individual actions to the historical incidents which provide the background, "transposing" the ideas generated in the play from men to nations, finally realizing that wars are simply further extensions of this same distortion of life.

In order to make the connection between the individual actions occurring on stage and the historical events, Adamov precedes each of his twelve scenes with brief comments from the 1900–1914 period. Using the methods of the political theater of Erwin Piscator, quotations from the newspapers and photographs of the major figures of the time are projected onto a screen, a technique which also functions as a means of "distancing" the action, breaking the illusion, and reminding the audience that it is in a theater. Each projection provides the necessary historical situation in which the characters move. As Paolo, Hulot-Vasseur, and Saulnier go through their paces, the spectator can link their actions to those related incidents on the social and political fronts; as the main characters proceed through their dramas, the spectator is able to connect them with the information he is given on the Boer War, the troubles in China, the struggle in Morocco, the Dreyfus affair, the Balkan War, the strikes in France, the effort to break the power of the unions. It is an easy step to relate Paolo's efforts to send Marpeaux from Venezuela to Morocco for his own business purposes to that of England exchanging Morocco for Egypt, both people and nations being used as articles of exchange. Most important, the projections on the screen help to convey the seriousness of the situation against which the frivolity of the people is contrasted. In his own remarks on the staging of *Paolo Paoli*, Adamov observed: "Do not forget the photos of Krupp and of Schneider. . . . I only placed butterflies and feathers on stage, but the screen must come forth with the representatives of capitalism, the faces of those responsible, visible, identified, named."[33] All of this culminates in the final set of projections, representing August, 1914, when Nicholas II of Russia is reported as saying to his cousin William II of Germany: "I imagine that you will be forced to mobilize," signifying the start of World War I.

In order to deal with this complex historical plot, Adamov adopted an entirely new method of work: He undertook extensive research and documentation on his subject. Up to this time, the playwright had drawn largely upon his own inner world and external matters were not probed. Starting with *Paolo Paoli* and continuing with his next few plays, Adamov concentrated on enriching his theater through a careful study of the people and their historical period: "I feared for a while that I was going to drown in documentation. Reading *The Century, The Free World, The Cross*, of course, *The Figaro* [newspapers of the period] in massive doses is rather maddening. But, little by little, a main idea asserted itself: exchange, merchandise."[34] The dramatist no longer felt that his work could advance without some external awareness, because, by now, he was arriving at a new concept of poetry which would come from facts, details which no imagination could supply: "Poetry, the true poetry, is always linked to the most extreme particularization."[35] In his view the allegorical aspects of the avant-garde and his former theater represented the opposite of what art should be; the true aesthetics of drama come from a study of time, place, and background.

His research led him into a deeper understanding not only of the capitalist system, but of those whom he saw as its victims: the powerless, the politically and economically impotent. In his new phase, the author came into contact with two groups which he considered to be the only audience capable of appreciating his writings: the workers and the youth. In his future plays he would keep these people in mind and, at times, they would play a central role in the works.

Paolo Paoli was first presented in Lyon at the Théâtre de la Comédie by Roger Planchon on May 24, 1957. Planchon, who had previously directed *Professor Taranne* and *The Direction of the March*, was actually Jacquie's choice. The playwright was enormously pleased with the final results, admiring the inventive creativity of the director as well as the effectiveness of the acting and the sets. It was at this time that the close association of the director and dramatist developed. The production, unfortunately, was not without its troubles. Planchon had at first been advised by one of the members of the Commission of Arts and Letters not to perform the play, with the veiled threat that Planchon would not obtain the subsidy needed to open up a theater which he had been planning in Villeurbanne, outside Lyon (*HE*, pp. 122–23). However, thanks to the intervention of Jacques Lemarchand, the drama critic of the *Figaro Littéraire*, the performance was permitted. Similar problems awaited the play in Paris, where it was the first such spectacle put on by Planchon in that city. Roger Martin du Gard, a major novelist and former Nobel Prize winner, had to intervene to insure the presentation. Despite the succession of obstacles, Adamov saw the production as a great triumph: "Public success of *Paolo Paoli*. The C.G.T.[36] and the Communists help us, it is true. All the seats are taken 10 days ahead of time. But the bourgeoisie, for its part, is impressed and attends" (*HE*, pp. 124–25).

In his new style, Adamov did not completely abandon the theater of the absurd, still retaining the grotesque and ridiculous situations, the exaggeration of detail, the inventive use of time. What he achieved, rather, was a fusion of the avant-garde with the epic, historical play, emphasizing the latter. As he indicated, he was well aware that the human condition contained both that which could be corrected by man's will and that which could not be changed. In his view, the only true theater was one which would take into account both aspects of life to create a total picture. Is this new approach more valid than his previous style? It seems likely that it is not, if the final answer is to be found in the effectiveness of the plays as presented in a theater. The early plays, whatever their deficiencies, conveyed a genuine expression of anguish and possessed a ring of truth which came from the depths of his soul. *Paolo Paoli* is an often brilliantly conceived and executed drama, providing incisive reflections on man in a social, political, and economic world, but it is also a strident, somewhat didactic, politically-biased theater. As such, it loses much of its power.

IV *The Short Plays*

In the years 1958–1960, Adamov's political commitment included not only his theater, but his personal life. May 13, 1958, was the turning point: "The Fascists have taken control in Algiers. Hoisted on their shoulders, smiling, satisfied de Gaulle rises again" (*HE*, p. 127). From that moment on, he would wage a struggle in defense of the Algerian people against de Gaulle. Jacquie entered the Communist party and, although Adamov did not follow suit, he participated with the Communists in demonstrations against the government. Lining himself up with what he called the non-Communist intellectual group (among whom he included Jean-Paul Sartre and Simone de Beauvoir), he fought actively against what he considered the injustices of the new regime, and he particularly campaigned against the Gaullist constitution. He also signed the "manifesto of the 121," a defense of the F.L.N.[37] terrorism, a reply to what he termed the "savage French aggression." However, he added, "all those who signed the manifesto can no longer work in radio or television. Fortunately, German and English friends come to our aid and give us work. We will not die of hunger" (*HE*, p. 136). Nevertheless, his personal life took a turn for the worse; in *Man and Child*, he talked about difficulties between himself and Jacquie, and, for the first time, mentioned the excessive drinking which was to take such a heavy toll on him as the years went along: "I am getting into the habit of drinking beer right away in the morning. . . . Nevertheless, my anguish increases. I drink more and more" (*HE*, p. 136).

Yet he continued to work, and his writing reflected his political concerns. During this period he was mainly involved in preparing *Le Printemps 71*, a play about the days of the 1871 Commune uprising in Paris. In doing the research for the drama, which will be discussed in the next section, he also compiled an *Anthology of the Commune* (1959), a collection of articles originally published in 1871 during the uprising. Adamov prepared this anthology because of his admiration for the people of the Commune and because he wanted to make his readers aware of a time when the working class had power. He hoped to explain the real situation of the Commune, especially indicating the prodigious amount of work required to make the city of Paris function during its period of control. It was also his intention to present the ferocity and baseness of the bourgeoisie and the people at Versailles.[38] It was his wish that all intellectuals recognize that the Spring of 1871, with the revolt of the Commune, contained the same elements as the Spring of 1959, suggesting the continued possibility of rebellion.

At the same time, the author kept himself active with a number of translations: Maxim Gorki's *The Enemies*, *The Mother*, and *The Petit Bourgeois*; Strindberg's *The Father*, as well as Chekhov's theater. He also adapted Nikolai Gogol's *Dead Souls* to the stage. Planchon presented his adaptation at the Théâtre de la Cité in Villeurbanne on January 22, 1960, and later in Paris at the Théâtre de l'Odéon on April 21 of the same year. Adamov saw Gogol's work as a mixture of sharp social criticism and poetry, involving the real and the unreal, which fitted into his own special vision of theater: "We have to find a theater which is absolutely *set in a specific direction* and absolutely *open*, which would show the real connection between the so-called dream world and the objective world. These two worlds are joined together in Gogol's book."[39]

During these years, he was also active composing four short plays which reflected his newly-developed political orientation as well as his strongly anti-Gaullist views. The first three, published in 1958 under the title *Théâtre de Société (Scènes d'Actualité)*, were written while Adamov was vacationing in Toulon with Guy Demoy and Maurice Regnault, friends of his who also contributed short plays to the publication. This was Adamov's first political theater satirizing current leaders and events. As such, it is important to note that the dramatist did not write solely in a realistic style, but also used allegory to make his point, clearly merging realistic expression with the world of fantasy. The purpose of the plays, according to the dramatist, was to draw a picture of France upon the arrival of de Gaulle: "The current situation, for example, with its apparent paradoxes, its grotesque reversals concealing the impeccable logic of class interests, must be *represented* as literally as possible, therefore as crudely as possible."[40]

In the first and best of these three one-act plays, *Intimité (Intimacy)*, Adamov uses a figurative treatment to show the collusion between de Gaulle and the various factions with which he dealt upon his return to power: big business, the moneyed class, and those agitating for continuation of French control in Algeria. Most of the characters in the work are personifications of pressure groups: Uves Borges de Ponteville and Monsieur Royal represent the aristocracy as well as the capitalist system; the Algerian *colons* (colonists) are depicted by Jean-Claude, an intolerant, arrogant ruffian, the nephew of de Ponteville; the enslaved people are caricatured in "Pupille," a weak, ineffectual servant, the lackey of the others; de Gaulle himself is presented in the form of "The Cause Incarnate," a vain, pompous man who enjoys listening to his voice on a record proclaiming that he is France and that he has saved the country. In close touch with the various groups, he is influenced by the money of big business and the noise created by the bullying tactics of the French settlers. One character sees the situation for its real value: "The Man Who Sees the Causes and Feels the Effects," the worker, the intellectual. However, he is attacked by the strong-arm bodyguards who protect "The Cause Incarnate," and the play ends with the de Gaulle and big business figures observing that rhythm is the touchstone of government, while the bodyguards beat up the worker.

A second play, *Je ne suis pas Français* (*I am not French*), also deals with the Algerian problem. Set in Algiers on May 14 or 15, 1958, during the "revolutionary" hours, the play is a satire on the manner in which the French paratroopers were said to have forced the Moslems in Algiers to demonstrate for the French government. In the first scene, the father of a *pied-noir* family (Algerians of European descent), becomes angry at an Algerian Moslem who accidentally bumps him, but he is told by one of the soldiers that there are new orders since May 13[41] and that the French are now obliged to fraternize with the Moslems. Throughout the play, these French paratroopers keep repeating to the Algerian natives: "Don't you know French? We will teach it to you, if you want," the sentences conveying the real meaning: the threat of continued French domination over the country and the people. In the second scene, following a demonstration by the Moslems on May 16, it is clear that the policy of fraternization is not working and the Moslems are being sought out for punishment by the French soldiers. In the final tableau, two English journalists are at first surprised to see so many Moslems at a pro-French rally, but soon they surmise correctly that the Moslems have been forced to attend and that they are unwilling participants. Inquiring further into the matter, the two journalists ask several of the Algerian residents what they think of the events of May 13. The answer is the same in all cases: "I am not French," indicating their bitter resentment of the French and their control. Adamov later criticized this play, calling it too schematic and too avant-garde. However, it now seems to be too realistic and not allegorical enough, the obviousness of its point of view and the slightness of its presentation being unfortunately emphasized by the realism of the work.

In the last of the three works, Adamov wrote a short monologue entitled *La Complainte du Ridicule* (*The Lament of Ridicule*), in which the playwright personifies Ridicule, which bemoans the fact that it is too tired and too old to kill with words as it did in the past. Today, with the new Gaullist constitution, it has too much to do. If the people will stand up and say "no" to the Republic, Ridicule will function effectively once again. Written in September, 1958, this slender sketch was meant to be a response to de Gaulle's referendum for a new constitution.

The playwright continued his attack on the new political regime with one more short play: *Les Apolitiques* (*The Apolitical People*), published in December, 1958. The subject for the work probably came out of an anti-Gaullist demonstration in which Adamov participated on September 4, 1958, following which Adamov, Jacquie, and Simone de Beauvoir entered a café. After they had taken a seat, a number of workers came in, beaten and bloodied by the police, according to Adamov, who added: "Our café opened its doors to let the wounded in, others won't do as much" (*HE*, p. 129). The action of *The Apolitical People* takes place in the café, Le Crébillon, on Friday, May 30, 1958. The customers in the café, while discussing politics, generally proclaim their indifference to and disdain for the subject. However, their actions soon contradict this statement. A well-dressed Algerian enters the café and the proprietor promptly tells him that he must pay in advance before he can be served. Camille, one of the customers and the Adamov spokesman in the work, offers to pay for him, feeling that the owner's request is a gross injustice. A student then comes in, identified in the stage directions as "perhaps Communist, perhaps Jewish, perhaps both, perhaps neither one nor the other, who, in any event, is reading *L'Humanité* [the Communist newspaper]."[42] The others, except Camille, begin to criticize the student for trying to sell the newspaper. Suddenly two Fascists burst into the café, tear up the paper, and start beating the student. Camille is horrified, saying that totalitarianism is very near, opening the door so that the audience hears the noises of car horns, symbolizing the activities of the Fascists pursuing their opponents. In this short and generally insignificant work, Adamov is trying to indicate how fascism has swept the entire country, whether it be in the Gaullist regime or in the fight to retain Algeria.

In point of fact, most of these short plays have a lackluster quality. It is most likely that they did not require much effort from the author and were written for specific, temporary purposes rather than out of a real conviction. One of the dramatist's major strengths has always been the capacity to convey deep emotions to the audience, a characteristic generally missing in these works. At the same time, the length of these short pieces also works against them. The Adamovian world, whether dreamlike or realistically committed, is so special in its peculiar, oblique vision that the spectator-reader cannot enter and appreciate it in plays that run only seven or eight pages; the mood created by the dramatist demands more extensive expression.

V *"Puppet Shows" and Reality*: Le Printemps 71 (Spring 71)

The same criticisms cannot be leveled against Adamov's next play, *Le Printemps 71* (*Spring 71*). His major literary effort during the years 1958–1960, this work represents a significant commitment on his part. Divided into twenty-six scenes, nine interludes, and an epilogue, *Spring 71* is an intricate portrayal of the uprising of the Paris Commune[43] in 1871 and its eventual tragic suppression. A minutely-observed account, the play took three years to write and required a vast amount of research: "I am gathering material for *Spring 71*. The periodical room at the National Library once more. I read numerous newspapers of the Commune and of Versailles. I am beginning to learn by heart everything which took place between March 18 and May 31, 1871" (*HE*, p. 131). When he had finished writing, in the Winter of 1960, Adamov realized that the piece contained about forty characters: "Who will produce this play, not only antibourgeois, aggressive, but, moreover, costing a fortune? Megalomaniac that I am, I will be punished" (*HE*, p. 138).

It is clear that Adamov intended this extensive work as a major advance in his writing. Like *Paolo Paoli*, *Spring 71* does not have any direct connection with his neuroses but concentrates rather on the *mal curable*, the social evils which can be changed. Written in a spirit of indignation not only over the events in Algeria, but over the massacres in Madagascar,[44] and especially over what Adamov termed the *mascarade* of Republican government, this new work was meant to be an accurate evocation of man and his place in the historical and social milieu around him. To a great extent, Adamov's violent reaction to the political events surrounding him, with the reemergence of de Gaulle and, in Adamov's view, his Fascist government, took the place of his own personal obsessions and diverted him temporarily from his inner torments.

Spring 71 is the natural progression of the playwright's evolution away from strictly avant-garde theater. After deliberately turning from the theater of the absurd, he wrote *Ping-Pong*, a first attempt to link his sense of internal alienation with an external situation, through the image of the pinball machine. *Paolo Paoli* was a further step in this direction, dealing with big business and war, although the major events were suggested through the seven characters who appeared in the play rather than being presented on stage. *Spring 71* is an attempt to treat the historical event directly, to let the audience see and understand by a documented approach what took place: "In that manner, I could also finally get out of those 'interiors,' where I was smothering, and not only could the bourgeois speak, but everybody could speak, those who are the majority in the world, that is, whether one likes it or not, the proletarians" (*Th*, IV, 87). His theater was now aimed at the working class and this group took center stage. Like Marpeaux in *Paolo Paoli*, the worker was the main character and was represented many times over in the numerous characters in the play.

The idea for the drama came to Adamov a few years earlier when he was reading an illustrated book on the Commune of Paris. He was fascinated by the account and began to study the period in more detail, learning what it was really like, so he said, rather than what the "Republican" history books recounted. He then felt that it was virtually his duty to write about this first government of the working class, "the courage, the intelligence, then the heroism which made Paris the capital of the world for three months, is that not one of the greatest subjects in the theater? And so many things touch me personally in this Commune that I cannot list them. So many things, and especially perhaps the total fraternity . . . the struggle, elbow to elbow."[45] The isolation of man confronted with unnamable forces, defeated by his own neuroses, was now partially replaced with the almost lyrical joy of the battle along with comrades and friends, with the realization that there are others with whom to share the burden of existence. It was this almost sentimental regard for people, particularly the common man, that Adamov wanted to convey, telling of men, women, children who "knew all possible feelings, who were raised beyond themselves, and all of this, of course, without always being able to avoid the sadness, the weakness, the cowardliness" (*Th.*, IV, 88). This was to be a drama of the ordinary people, the unknowns who became the heroes. This type of historical drama would be different from that associated with Schiller, Hugo, *et al.* Adamov's approach, he maintained, would be more realistic, his individuals more authentic.

Curiously, there was a period when he first began *Spring 71* during which Adamov was tempted to write the play without including any of the people of the Commune.[46] Having finished *Paolo Paoli*, and having realized that Marpeaux, the only "positive" character in the work, was not particularly well drawn, Adamov had a "momentary aberration" when he thought that he should not present characters with good qualities, that, like Brecht, rather than ask the public to accept a positive spectacle, he should try to get it to reject a negative spectacle, an approach which he had attempted in a limited way with his presentation of big business in *Paolo Paoli*. He soon abandoned the idea, however, and the introduction of the people of the Commune, the workers of Paris, and the obvious sympathetic treatment by Adamov demand the spectator's compassion, breaking with the Brechtian theory that the audience should not identify emotionally with the characters on stage.

As a matter of fact, Adamov was quite familiar with Brecht's play, *The Days of the Commune* (1948–1949), dealing with the same subject. He considered the Brecht drama a failure and stressed the fact that he could never have begun his own play if he had not been convinced of this. According to Adamov, Brecht had made a mistake in not trying to achieve a proper balance between the "great" events which made up the history of the period and the "small" events which constituted the individual's connection with this history.[47] In Adamov's view, it was because Brecht emphasized "History" at the expense of the individual that his play did not succeed. Adamov tried to create this proper balance, not allowing the audience to forget that it was watching an historical play based upon facts, while also giving the public an opportunity to link this history with the individual and his actions. In so doing, he drew upon a new source of inspiration, Sean O'Casey: "What I sometimes reproach Brecht for is the fact that the spectator does not sufficiently understand the characters. Of course, from the point of view of the breadth of his work, Brecht is the greatest writer in the theater of the XXth century. However, O'Casey has achieved something which touches me deeply: a much closer union between public life and private life."[48] Adamov especially felt that O'Casey's

Red Roses for Me had been a most remarkable fusion of the individual life with the social and political facts. In the play O'Casey tells the story of Ayamonn's visionary act of faith in a new world, a prophetic vision of life that will lead the people to a better future. O'Casey personalized the play by recounting the love of the Protestant Ayamonn for the Catholic Sheila. At the same time, their love was related to the social context of the railroad workers and their demands for a wage increase, leading to strikes, riots, and death.

This was now Adamov's approach to theater, showing the interreactions and interrelationships of individuals and historical events. In *Spring 71*, the subject lends itself unusually well to this theory. All of the personal activities of the characters—their joys, sorrows, triumphs, disasters—are a result of their involvement in the 1871 uprising, the factual basis of the play. This is what Bernard Dort calls "a theater of historical understanding, in which the great events and the daily lives clarify each other mutually."[49]

Adamov created this link between the private and public lives by a careful structuring of the play. In between the twenty-six scenes, he placed nine interludes called *guignols* (puppet shows). These *guignols* (not actually performed by puppets but by human beings) provide the historical framework in which the fictional or dramatic lives of the characters function. Each of the figures in the interludes represents one of the major historical characters or forces during the uprising: the German Chancellor Bismarck, seeking to extend his control over France; Adolphe Thiers, France's president, who uses any possible means to quell the Commune's revolt, even up to and including German support; the Bank of France, usually wrapped inside its vaults, worried about its money; the National Assembly, a grumpy, sleepy old lady knitting socks; the Mediator, who tries to find a common ground between the two groups and fails; the Commune itself, fighting for its life.

When he included these interludes, Adamov had two ideas in mind. He was first able to retain the Brechtian principle of alienation, to "distance" the play, to remind the audience that it was watching a spectacle and to bring it back to its own reality so that it could reflect upon what was taking place. Since the playwright sympathized with the people of the Commune and, inevitably, engendered the same sort of sympathy in the audience, the *guignols* served the necessary function of pulling the spectator abruptly back, placing matters in proper perspective. At the same time, the dramatist wanted these interludes to familiarize the public with the history of the Commune. By describing the events of the period in this somewhat caricatural and cartoon-like presentation, it was his hope that the spectators would be able to obtain enough of the necessary details to avoid elaborate and boring explanations in the realistic sections of the work. Inspired by Daumier, the *guignols* supplied the historical background as well as the caricatural quality of the leaders. Adamov expected that the style of acting in these interludes would contrast with that of the realistic scenes, with the actors delivering their lines as if they were reading a newspaper or reciting lines of poetry.[50]

Besides this distinction, the playwright also intended that, in the realistic sections of the play, there should be a differentiation between the *Versaillais* (the ruling class which had established itself in Versailles upon its flight from Paris) and the *Communards*. In providing directions to Otto Haas for the production in Czechoslovakia, Adamov noted: "The *Versaillais*... almost never move. Their voices swell or go down only to the extent that they are afraid, are less afraid or no longer have any fear at all. They are *almost not men*."[51] He warned, however, that they were not to be performed like the *guignols*, for they belonged to the personal or realistic scenes which he viewed as basically straightforward in presentation, emphasizing both the psychological and political elements.

Most of those who represent the establishment are shown as treacherous, deceptive, and, eventually, fearful of their lives. Once again, a conniving priest plays a central role, as he did in *Paolo Paoli*. The aristocrats flee to Versailles, displaying more concern for their property than for human decency. Upon their return to power, they show the same indifference to human problems, interested only in their own fiefdom, willing to pursue any of the necessary brutalities in order to regain power. To the charge that he was too harsh on the *Versaillais*, the writer responded: "All you have to do is to document yourself on the history of the Commune even in the most superficial manner to observe that my *Versaillais* and even my '*Versaillais* of the left' are discreet compared to their historical models."[52]

In this tribute to the working class, the hero or heroes of the occasion are the people of the Commune. In Adamov's view, there are no major nor minor characters—they all participate in the moments of triumph and defeat: Robert Oudet, editor of the newspaper,

Cri du Peuple; Léon Oudet, his father and a follower of Proudhon;[53] Jeanne-Marie, Robert's wife, who remains firm in her commitment to the movement; Pierre Fournier, her brother and a follower of Blanqui;[54] Tonton, a worker and member of the local commission; Polia, a nurse from Poland who comes to participate in the uprising; Sofia, a Russian student (the Russian-born Adamov did not forget the international flavor of the Commune). In the play's forty characters, most of whom are members of the movement, there is a real sense of life, of the passions and emotions of the people who participated in the event. However, according to the dramatist, the work was intended less as a hymn of praise to the *Communards* than as a realistic piece of criticism of the errors of the people. Although they are clearly presented as humane, kind, and sensitive, they are also shown in their harsher moments of frustration and, sometimes, cruelty.

While it is to Adamov's credit that many of the characters of the Commune are depicted in their times of weakness, it is less praiseworthy that his criticism of the "errors" of the people is based more on political blunders than on a lack of human decency. Robert Oudet is a case in point: If we had to name a "hero," Oudet would be chosen. It is he who is the voice of reason, who helps guide the people, who has the intelligence and the clear perspective to understand what is happening. It is also Oudet who does *not* try to persecute others who do not share his views, who does *not* seek revenge; he is the most compassionate of the group, the only character who has real sympathy for his fellowman. In his comments on the play, Adamov especially criticized the moderate position taken by Oudet, noting that the play could just as easily have been titled "The Political Errors of Robert Oudet." In this respect, the playwright obviously accepted the position that a revolution must use any possible means to achieve its goals, a change from his attitude toward the *Militant* in *The Maneuver*.

Actually, each of the characters, although part of a group, has his own individual identity and evolves throughout the play in relation to the political situation. Oudet, in Adamov's version, understands that he has made mistakes, and judges himself accordingly; Polia changes from the outsider who always participates in "great" causes to an accepted member of the Commune, a natural result of her having lived through the good and the bad moments; the café owner Mémère, a reluctant participant at the beginning, offers her silver so that it will help the revolutionary cause and then, following her son's death, changes her allegiance once again, betraying the group, out of fear for her surviving daughter.

Each character reacts differently to the events which involve him, and the resultant change is closely linked to the question of time, an essential aspect of the work. For it was the brief life of the Commune (seventy-three days) and the terrible lack of time amidst the increasing complexity and multiplication of events which also first attracted Adamov to the story: "This contraction of time allowed me to emphasize how, because of events, one person will become aware of political reality, while another will lose the little or the 'great deal' of awareness that he had" (*Th.*, IV, 88). The title itself conveys time's importance and its role in human lives. The dramatist wanted to show that the passage of the days was so rapid that the Commune could not complete its work before it was too late, that the swiftness of events made final success virtually impossible. The characters are never at the same point as the events taking place, they are always ahead or behind: Montmartre has already been taken by the *Versaillais* and the *Communards* are still saying that nothing has been lost because no one can take Montmartre; people are in despair over situations which have already been resolved by measures decreed by the insurgent government. It is therefore understandable that, like the pinball machine in *Ping-Pong* or the butterflies in *Paolo Paoli*, the object around which much of the activity takes place in this play is the newspaper, *Cri du Peuple*. The newspaper is the perfect symbol of the effect of time on people, the gap between event and knowledge. As Margaret Dietemann notes, "Just as a newspaper must of necessity be already behind the times when it goes to press, so in a sense the Commune was outdated before it was finished, and the people who struggled so hard for it, dead while still alive."[55] Adamov reacted strongly to this problem of time because the emotional effects on the people are so similar to the feelings which the dramatist experienced in life. Time, the lack of it, the terrible complexity of dealing with it, and the resultant defeat of the *Communards* at its hands are not that far removed from the situations of the characters in Adamov's early plays when they were confronted with the implacable force of destiny. It is thus interesting to observe that the playwright still retained a connection with the first phase of his writing, even in this, the most factual of all his plays. Although his emphasis was on the "curable" aspects of life, he intended that the audience understand that, no matter what situation man might find himself in, there was always the substratum of the *mal incurable* with which he must also cope.

Along with *Paolo Paoli*, *Spring 71* was one of Adamov's favorite plays and was the one work which he considered the most finished. A carefully documented undertaking, the play possesses a rich, vital energy, succeeding remarkably well in evoking the life of the *Communards*. Amidst the tragic situation in which they find themselves, ending in their massacre, the people retain a sense of gaiety, hope, and optimism. This feeling of optimism amidst tragedy and triumph over despair is probably the strongest emotion communicated in the piece. In Adamov's new theater, he planned to stress the great possibilities which life offered, in spite of the certainty of death. Because he was a highly emotional person, he could not follow the Brechtian formula and did allow the audience a feeling of recognition for the characters. But the *guignols*, with their alienating effect, provided the proper balance which the playwright sought between the small and the big events, also permitting the spectator to react intellectually as well as emotionally. Although it is true that the work is one-sided, that the *Communards* are the "noble" people much admired by the dramatist, this aspect is not excessive and does not seem to be much more than a point of view which any dramatist has the right to express. Most important, the people of the Commune have been given a sense of authenticity by the playwright, a realism which lends credence to their actions.

Yet, despite Adamov's passionate involvement and despite the air of reality surrounding the play, *Spring 71* is not successful. It is very difficult to accept Adamov's revolutionary fervor, which often clashes with the audience's normal feelings for human kindness: The spectator can only appreciate and feel compassion for Robert Oudet's moderate position and hope for a decent end to the bitter struggle. Further, the innumerable details and carefully researched documentation leave the public bewildered and confused most of the time. A person of excesses, Adamov gave the audience too much to understand and to absorb. The playwright became aware of this after he had finished the work: "Rereading *Spring 71* these days, I wondered if the play were not a little too complicated—too many themes mixed together, too many parallel or inverse psychological evolutions, in short, too much concern for presenting a total, exact image, day after day, of reality, from which one is constantly expected to draw fragmentary political lessons."[56]

Adamov finished writing the work in 1960 and the play was first published in the journal *Théâtre Populaire*. It was originally performed in June, 1962, in London and later that year in Czechoslovakia. On April 26, 1963, it was presented at the Théâtre Gérard Philipe in Saint-Denis, a strongly Communistic working-class suburb outside of Paris. Directed by Claude Martin, the play succeeded moderately well, although the critics were not especially pleased. Adamov, however, found it moving, but regretted that the sentimental side of the Commune, which he himself had already emphasized, had been stressed a little too strongly. An extremely difficult work to present and exceptionally long (it runs four hours), *Spring 71* was never again presented in its entirety in France, much to Adamov's sorrow.

CHAPTER 4

The Synthesis: Neurosis and Marxism

NO sooner had Adamov formulated his new political drama with its documentation and research, than he refined it and merged it with the avant-garde theater of his first phase. In 1962, he even went so far as to make the following observation: "The only certain basis is almost always neurosis. And I have not changed my mind. Marxist or non-Marxist, the only problem is to know *how to utilize one's neuroses.*"[1] Once having denounced the theater of the absurd as irrelevant and useless, Adamov recognized that it now seemed quite contradictory to accept it again. This did not prevent him, however, from seeing the new melding of his two styles as a further improvement of his drama: "I have joined, reunited, a little better than in the past, the psychology of the individual and the general, *political* line of everyone" (*Th.*, III, 9). As this statement implies, the playwright's two styles of writing had always been present in his writing. While *The Parody* utilized the police state atmosphere as part of its background, *One Against Another*, with its theme of the persecution of the Jews, was another significant move toward a politically-committed theater. On the other hand, the "political" plays, *Paolo Paoli* and *Spring 71*, were never completely removed from the avant-garde, with the projections of history and the *guignol* scenes providing their own form of alienation. Further, the question of time, so similar to the role of fate, played a major part in *Spring 71*. In his next two plays, *La Politique des restes* and *Sainte Europe*, Adamov would try out variations on his new union of the personal and the political.

I   *The Clinical Case and Racism:*
La Politique des restes (The Politics of Waste)

This play, written during the winter of 1961–1962, was the first play in which the dramatist made a conscious attempt to unite his two styles of writing. In a comment made in 1967, but speaking about his theater since *Spring 71*, Adamov (who at that time had been confined to a hospital for a serious illness) noted that the realm of the real and the world of the neuroses were the two vital elements necessary to his theater: "I now want to link the clinical case (two years of sickness; from hospitals to clinics I know the situation quite well) to the political situation, without either one being sacrificed; I want to connect the world of sickness with a hyphen to the world called real. I move from the individual to multiplicity."[2] In *The Politics of Waste*, the playwright had a perfect opportunity to test out his dramatic theory. The subject of the play, including the title, came from a clinical observation made by a Doctor Minkowski in the journal *Le Temps vécu*. Dr. Minkowski reported the case of an individual suffering from the psychosis of the multiplicity of things: too many seasons, too many days, too many trains, too many tickets, too many objects—wine bottles, cigarette butts, torn-up letters, etc.[3] The man, suffering from delusions of persecution as well as feelings of masochism, imagined that he was guilty of being a foreigner in France and of not having paid his taxes. Because of these supposed "crimes," he assumed that he would be punished, his arms and legs would be cut off, and he would be placed in a fair along with other wild beasts to be looked at and mocked. The patient had also developed what he called the "politics of waste." He thought that all the waste and refuse in the world were being put aside in order to be placed one day into his stomach.

This sense of persecution and masochism of the foreigner in France obviously struck a responsive chord in Adamov, who could certainly appreciate much of the suffering involved. The playwright had already used this type of clinical observation as the basis of one of his short radio plays, *En Fiacre* (*In the Cab*), but, in that work, the events were linked only to the psychosis itself. In *The Politics of Waste*, Adamov, now definitely committed to the idea that theater must also say something about the world in which man lives, felt that the clinical case was not a sufficiently large topic. Once having created his central character, Johnnie Brown (like his real-life counterpart, he is frightened about the general multiplicity of things), the dramatist then placed the action in a specific country, South Africa, "where the Whites are suffering with fear, but not because of the *general* multiplicity of things, but only because of the *particular* multiplicity of 'Negroes' " (*Th.*, III, 8). The playwright attempted to show that the individual neurosis is closely linked to the collective neurosis, that the sickness of the individual leads to collective injustice. In the play, Johnnie moves from a fear of waste or refuse to a fear of the Blacks, because they too in his mind are so numerous and so prolific. From that point he develops the idea that it is the Blacks who are responsible for the refuse, and he takes the final step by killing a Black man.

The scene of the play is a courtroom in which Johnnie Brown, an industrialist, is accused of having killed Tom Guinness, a Black. During the trial, while the lawyers for the defense and prosecution present their cases, flashbacks intermingle with the testimony of the witnesses to explain what took place. One of the witnesses, Doctor Perkins, observes that Johnnie has just recently been released from a clinic where he was being treated for his illness. Johnnie maintains that his wife, Joan, and brother, James, are persecuting him and that they had him placed in the clinic in order to have a free hand in merging his company with a cartel. Like the patient on whom Adamov modeled his play, Johnnie is hostile to the world, knowing that all the waste of the earth is being "put aside to be placed into my belly one day. All the refuse of the world, of the universe, everything, you understand? . . . the fruit pits, the chicken bones, the wine and water which stagnate in the bottom of glasses" (*Th.*, III, 156). In Adamov's view, Johnnie's fears are not so irrational when one thinks of the situation in South Africa where the Whites are in a definite minority and hence have a similar fear of the proliferation of Blacks. Johnnie's wife and brother are also terrified, Joan recounting the tale that one day a number of Blacks surrounded her and put their hands over her body. Luis Galao, Johnnie's barber, was afraid to enter Johnnie's house because he saw some Blacks outside holding a funeral procession; they are all frightened of being "swept away, eaten up in no time at all." It thus becomes obvious that Johnnie's fear of waste and then of Blacks is only a part of society's own terrors, and his case is not so much an isolated example as a representation of the social system at large.

It is now the social system which is on trial, and the oppressiveness of its nature becomes steadily evident. In effect, the court of law becomes a microcosm of the racism that exists in the Whites. The lawyer for the prosecution, understanding this, does not ask for the full punishment for Johnnie, because "this state of nerves, this heated anger, this illegitimate and . . . reprehensible exercise of violence were essentially dictated to him by a sensitive, exaggerated, although misguided, I grant you, but sincere concern, a concern not only for his own interests, but also for the legitimate interests of our

State" (*Th.*, III, 178). As a result, the prosecutor asks for a light sentence.

Johnnie and his lawyer become enraged. In his defense statement, the lawyer argues that Johnnie killed only one Black and that Blacks die all the time, either by diseases like tuberculosis, or more frequently, at the hands of the police or other Whites. Upon hearing this and realizing its full import, Johnnie then transfers his neuroses from the dread of the Blacks to a fear of his fellow white men. He imagines that if the Whites are allowed to get away with killing the Blacks, they could just as well do the same thing to him. He therefore declares that he will defend himself against them and kill any and all. At this, the Court is thunderstruck and, immediately, the prosecuting attorney asks that Johnnie be sent back to the asylum: "It is not necessary to be a psychiatrist to declare formally that any white person ready to kill other Whites under the pretext that one day the latter would seek a quarrel with him, that such a man is sick and even dangerously sick" (*Th.*, III, 185).

The Politics of Waste is a mixture of the old and the new for Adamov. In Doctor Minkowski's patient, the playwright found someone who shared many of his own neuroses and Johnnie bears the same masochistic tendencies that have appeared in previous Adamov characters: the Kafkaesque fear of being swept away, of being nothing but refuse. In the final analysis, "N." of *The Parody* suffers the same fate when he is swept off the stage like "household filth"; the *Mutilé* in *The Maneuver* is also nothing but an object at the end of the play; and Pierre in *The Invasion* is shattered by the multiplicity of people invading his world. The playwright once again has made his obsessions an integral part of his writing, just as they remained so strongly a part of his personal life. Yet, this time, the individual neurosis is more clearly a part of the collective action with the personal torment linked to a much broader anguish. The play, while a presentation of Johnnie's irrational fears, is also a strong indictment of the class system. That is why Adamov preferred to tell the story through the form of a trial, because the effect of Johnnie's statements on the others is more telling than the analysis of the crime itself. Essentially, Adamov suggests, Johnnie's crime is less important than the actions of society, particularly societies like those of South Africa or the United States with their racial prejudice. It is clear that Johnnie will not be punished for killing a Black—he is White and belongs to the ruling class (in this respect, class and race are the same thing). While his crime may be strikingly overt, it is nonetheless not much different from the crimes being perpetrated by those in power. It follows, then, that the courts cannot hand out justice, since the people in charge of the courts have the same prejudices: They realize that Johnnie's actions are only an externalization of their own sentiments. Such a class system reacts only when it sees the hatred directed against itself, and that is why it cannot tolerate Johnnie's final decision to kill Whites; he must be placed in an asylum. All levels of society contribute to Johnnie's incarceration, all of them willing accomplices: James, representing big business; Joan, the daughter of a pastor of the Dutch Reformed Church; even Johnnie's own lawyer; and Doctor Perkins, symbolizing the field of medicine, which allies itself with the law to rid society of anyone who might endanger the *status quo*.

Although the action of the play supposedly takes place in South Africa, it could also occur in a southern American state, as Adamov indicated in his stage directions. In 1959, the dramatist made the first of two trips to the U.S., this time to see a production of *Ping-Pong* being performed Off Broadway. While there, he was invited to visit a rich businessman in New York, whose wife spoke French: "She tells me that she never goes to Harlem but that she is sad about it. She 'loves' the Negroes very much, but they don't love her, what can she do?" (*HE*, p. 133). At that point, a young child entered with a black nurse. Adamov asked the woman: "If you think that the Negroes hate you, why do you keep a Negro to watch over your child?" Her answer: "But because Negroes love children so much." She adds, suddenly speaking English: "When they are not together, they are not dangerous" (*HE*, p. 133).[4] This visit to the United States and his experiences with the country's social system were undoubtedly a major source of *The Politics of Waste*.

Another source was Brecht's *The Exception and the Rule*, written in 1930. In this play, which Adamov knew very well, a Chinese merchant mistakes an action of kindness by a coolie for a threat, killing the coolie. At a subsequent trial, the judge finds that the merchant had every reason to expect that the coolie would hate him and, therefore, he was simply acting in legitimate self-defense. The parallel with Adamov's trial scene is striking enough to leave little doubt that the Brecht play was an important inspiration for Adamov.

Brecht's influence is also evident in the structure. While the trial is superficially realistic, it is soon evident that Adamov is using the Brechtian effect of alienation. Throughout the testimony of the witnesses, Johnnie constantly intervenes, arguing his own case, so that the sense of realism is destroyed and the play seems very much like the fable that it is. More significantly, Adamov utilizes flashbacks to tell the story, intermingling scenes from the past with those of the present. Like the *guignols*, these flashbacks provide the necessary background to the story and also distance the action. At the same time, they take place on an elevated podium at the front of the stage, reflecting the dramatist's intention to use the stage in its widest possible means of expression, constantly trying out new techniques.

The dramatist was not entirely satisfied with *The Politics of Waste* in its final form because he felt that the subject of racism required a more extensive presentation and that the concept of waste could have been expanded to encompass a broader political spectrum. Despite Adamov's cavils, *The Politics of Waste* is a viable work. Less ambitious than subsequent plays, the limited direct sphere of action and concentration of point of view may be more successful than the later, more complex works. The connection between the individual and collective neuroses is well made, and the innovative staging makes the piece a striking, although minor, drama.[5]

II Ici et maintenant (Here and Now)

Adamov did not finish another play for four years because of poor health, but he did compile *Ici et maintenant* (*Here and Now*), a collection of his comments on theater. This collection, published in 1964, is composed of two parts: The first, and longer, groups together various observations made by the dramatist about his own plays, either via prefaces to his works or through extended articles in newspapers and journals; the second part contains Adamov's analyses of the writers or theater people whom he admired and who had influenced him: Strindberg, Brecht, Chekhov, O'Casey, Piscator, Gorki.

The essays in *Here and Now*, which were written from 1950 until January of 1964, provide a fairly complete picture of the progression and evolution of Adamov's thinking about his own theater and theater in general. Since the texts are arranged chronologically, it is easy to follow his thought processes as he moved from his "eternal" drama of dreamlike sequences to that which he called "a theater which, modestly, tries to give an account of the real difficulties of life—political, psychological, even psychiatric."[6] In the course of this study, many of his comments from *Here and Now* have already been extensively cited in the discussion of the plays. However, in October of 1962, he mentioned a new play that he was considering, a work which was never written but whose outline reflects his concept of theater.

He planned to write *La Chanson des malheureux* (*The Song of the Unfortunate*), which would take place in the Germany of the Weimar Republic during the years 1930–1933, a time of unemployment and economic crisis as well as the period of the rise of Nazism. The small milieu of the intellectuals was to be the center of the action, and most of the characters were to have something to do with the Expressionist theater. Using the Pirandellian technique of the play-within-a-play, Adamov envisioned the work as functioning on three levels: (1) real life, the life of "those days"; (2) the realm of art, the "refuge"; (3) the political arena. Within these levels, several new and old themes would be emphasized: masochism, the major theme; sexual perversion; the sadism and fetishism which existed during those years in Germany; the contrast between man's image of death and the real death; the Jewish question; the relationship of the Nazis with big businesses like the Krupp and Thyssen empires; the help which the Nazis received from London, New York, and Paris. Although the play was never written, Adamov's outline gives a clear idea of the dramatist's intention of continuing to merge the personal with the historical, the psychological with the political, an intention that seemed to be uppermost in his mind in 1964.

After having finished rereading *Here and Now*, Adamov wrote a postscript in which he observed that his writing had not really expressed what he had wanted to say, namely, that the theater must force itself to discuss both individual and collective lives: "Anything which does not link man to his own phantoms, but also, and even more so, to other men, and at that point, to the phantoms of other men, and all of this in a given, nonimaginary period, anything which does not do this does not have the slightest interest, either philosophically or artistically."[7] Adamov's future orientation was settled. He would now develop his aesthetics of drama, mixing his own dosage of Strindberg, the theater of the absurd, Brecht, O'Casey, and Marxism. His future endeavors, as René Gaudy notes, would be a blending of *Professor Taranne* and *Spring 71*.[8]

III   *A Satire of the Western World:* Sainte Europe (Holy Europe)

It took Adamov almost three years to finish *Sainte Europe* (*Holy Europe*). He began the work in 1963, but his emotional and physical conditions were beginning to worsen rapidly: "My anguish is such that, up until noon, it is impossible for me not only to work, but even to make the slightest gesture, to unfold a newspaper for example. . . . I have to drink at least three bottles of German beer and one or two gins in order to get into the coming day" (*HE*, pp. 151–52). In spite of the fact that he was not able to escape his torment and his deteriorating physical state, he did manage to make another trip to the United States where he gave courses at Cornell University and renewed his acquaintance with the country. Upon his return to France, he finished *Holy Europe* in 1966, but his situation was extremely bad: "I am drinking more and more, my mind is wandering. I have night dreams which frighten me; they already have a tendency to merge with my real life" (*HE*, p. 158).

Such a development could not help but affect his writing. *Holy Europe* is a fantastic, irrational, and bitter play; a mixture of mock-epic scenes and allegorical dream sequences, the drama is a terrifying indication of the author's view of the world. Adamov took the *guignols* of *Spring 71* and, making them the center of the work, created in *Holy Europe* a cartoon, a caricature of our world, particularly of the "free" Western world. Even more specifically, it is a violent, very often cruel attack on the leaders, especially on the dramatist's favorite target, Charles de Gaulle. Written with venom and anger, the play is an acid satire of the modern period, told under the guise of the Middle Ages. Karl, the de Gaulle figure, emperor of the "Frank" country, of "Alémanie," and of Castile, plans a crusade to the East, supposedly in the name of Christianity. In actual fact, Karl's aims are quite different: The crusade is designed both as an exercise in colonial diplomacy so that the Emperor will have a market for his goods, and as a diversionary tactic for the military, in order to prevent a coup.

Adamov intended this as a satire of the de Gaulle regime: "This age, or more specifically this regime in this age, which hides and disguises itself under the tinsel of another age: namely, the Middle Ages. And all of that in order to reach small sordid goals (of course)."[9] The play was also meant to be an indictment of the recently-formed Common Market, which the dramatist called "imperialist integration," and which he saw as being American dominated. Unlike *Paolo Paoli* and *Spring 71*, his previous political plays, there are no "positive" characters, no one from what he termed the "real population," i.e., the people or the working class. The figures are to be like *guignols*, ignoble puppets who govern the countries. And, like the *guignols*, although they are dealing with reality, they are cartoon-like characters whose essential absurdity becomes a visible representation of Adamov's view of the Western world, in which power, greed, and profit are the main goals.

With the Middle Ages as the ostensible setting, Adamov was ready to make a comment on the modern period: Karl, the Emperor ("Very tall in appearance, very austere or very fat, imbued with his own importance in any case"), is de Gaulle and, at the same time, he is also Charlemagne or Charles V;[10] Grethe-France-Laure, Karl's daughter, could represent modern-day France; Crépin le Petit, the King of Brabant (or Belgium), is the President of the North-Central-Southern European Republican Confederation, Adamov's fanciful name for the Common Market; his wife, Teresa, is another symbol of Belgium; and Honoré de Rubens is one of the important bankers in any age. Given the circumstances in which he tried to combine the modern and medieval in an allegorical form as a statement on de Gaulle and company, the dramatist wondered if he should try to show this group of people "as it is presented to us in the newspapers . . . or else should I give it, let us say, bizarre words and attitudes, contradicting in any case . . . the idea that our governments and their hired press would like us to have? I do not know."[11]

The playwright solved the problem by dividing the work into two alternating sections, the "realistic" scenes and the dream sequences. This is similar to the technique which he had already used in *Spring 71*, with one major difference: in *Holy Europe, all* his scenes are variations on the absurdity of reality. Even the so-called "realistic" scenes are often so nonsensical that they become examples of the theater of the ridiculous. The figures speak in a bombastic tone, a parody of normal speech, a style designed to mask their true intentions, purposely out of touch with reality; and the actions of the characters are ludicrous and farcical, possessing a fantastic quality, a not-so-subtle commentary by the dramatist on the credibility of governement leaders.

The dream sequences, a heightened form of this unreality, play an important role. Besides the obvious distancing technique (not particularly needed since the scenes of reality are enough of a distancing device in themselves), these sequences reveal the reactionary motives of the characters, contrasting sharply with the liberal statements which they make in the other scenes. Providing an allegorical comment upon the story, the dream passages take off the layers of hypocrisy with which the modern political world covers itself. Karl's dream is one of power in which he sees himself as Charlemagne being crowned by the Pope. He is the great Christian warrior struggling against the Bolsheviks, sending all those in his kingdom who disagree with him to fight the "Asiatics." Teresa, the strongly Catholic daughter of Honoré de Rubens and the first wife of Crépin, dreams that she is a Mother Superior of a convent or St. Theresa of Avila. However, her sense of religion in the dream is quite distorted: She is in love with Jesus Christ and, in Adamov's version, the sexual implications of her religion and of religion in general are made quite evident.[12] In Honoré de Rubens' dream, big business and money play the major parts; he imagines commercial enterprises in the Orient, buying and selling his way to success.

These dream sequences provide the basic themes of *Holy Europe*. Adamov's view of the Western world is one in which power, religion, and money play the key roles, all of them closely allied and intermingled, each one having its own important place in the capitalistic society, all contributing to the exploitation of the workers and of the weak and underdeveloped countries. The playwright sets this bitter and ironic tone in the prologue when Gregorian music is heard in the background while, off-stage, a voice purporting to be that of St. Bernard, promoter of the Second Crusade, is extolling the virtues of the Christian life in which man dies while fighting for his religion. The music then changes to a blending of *Deutschland über alles* and the *Chant des Africains*, and the voice is now that of a German general who is urging the French to come join his troops in fighting Bolshevism: "Long live our Guide in the fight against Asiatic Bolshevism: Adolf Hitler. Long live a happy France in a united Europe" (*Th.*, III, 192). Finally, the music switches to an air from the Elizabethan period and *M. le Prologue* steps forth to honor the merchants who do so much good for the country.[13]

In these opening remarks, Adamov is setting the stage for his comic masquerade and charade of Western civilization. Medieval man, suggests the dramatist, used the Crusades for supposedly noble ends, when in reality he was often only interested in extending his powers. Modern man does the same thing; his quest for control will be masked under the words of the struggle against atheism and against the Bolsheviks, and it will become a battle for the survival of Christianity and the free world. All of the characters, like those in *Paolo Paoli*, are dealers in humanity—they utilize people in order to increase their own business empires. Their world is deceitful, full of threats, and completely lacking in any sense of morality. When Karl learns that the Americans have used the atomic bomb in Iran, he is not upset because of the moral issue of the use of the bomb; he is furious because he was not informed about the plan ahead of time. Like many real-life leaders, his ego is often more important than the issue involved.

The picture that the playwright draws is of crude, coarse, and vulgar people. When Karl receives the Agha of Iranie, Iran, and Jordanie and his wife on an official state visit, the Agha becomes completely inebriated (a state in which he will remain throughout the rest of the play). Rubens gives the Agha's wife a present with which she is delighted: a pair of shoes, equipped with bulb and battery to glow in the dark. Once again, religion and the United States come in for their share of the criticism. The "liberal" Pope is represented as an opportunistic cynic who jumps on the bandwagon of the new Ecumenical movement: He plans to give his tiara to the "Sanctuary of the Immaculate Conception of the Black, Venezuelan and Semi-Indian Catholic University." However, before he does so, he will display it at "Yankee-End-et-Jewish Stadium" to express his gratitude to the American people. Mr. Henderson, the ambassador from "North-Central-South America" has an even better idea: He will auction off the tiara so that more money will be raised to "help the poor." America, the constant thorn in the side of Karl, the de Gaulle character, is shown as the power behind the throne, the source of most of the financial aid to Europe and the real supporter of the Common Market.

All of these grotesque characters are walled up within their own essentially small, albeit powerful, worlds, completely out of touch with the reality surrounding them, with no awareness of the people's needs or wants. In order to get the workers to produce more, they lower the salaries and are then surprised when the workers are unhappy. Throughout the play there is a constant background of trouble: strikes, mine and flood disasters, revolts. Yet, all of this difficulty seems far away and does not disrupt the celebration of

Karl and his friends; in fact, Adamov wants this continual unrest and trouble in the world to contrast with the willful indifference of the leaders. As a result, at the end of the play, the people finally revolt and the cries of "Freedom" are heard, signaling a termination to the cruelty of their leaders.

In Adamov's view, the leaders of Western Europe and America—the free world—are hypocritical, their lives a sham. The main indication of their duplicity is seen in their language and patterns of speech. Grotesque, insincere, hollow, their dialogue reeks of jargon borrowed for the occasion, ranging from the "aesthetic" artificiality of the Pope to the empty pragmatism of the American Ambassador, Mr. Henderson. Each character has his own style, a parody of the rhetoric of the pressure group which he represents: Karl is the perfect mock example of de Gaulle's speeches, full of the royal "We," innumerable subordinate clauses, imperfect subjunctives, and excessively structured sentences; the Pope patterns his speech after the Ecumenism of the day; Honoré de Rubens recalls the newspapers with their superficially liberal attitudes, but betraying their essentially business-like approach.[14] Besides the contrived rhetoric of the scenes of reality, the characters in the dream sequences express themselves in a form of doggerel verse, the comic and burlesque rhymes revealing even more their basic foolishness. Their lives are a masquerade of reality, and Adamov climaxes the play with a masked ball, a sort of masquerade upon a masquerade, in which the puppet-like figures expose their fundamental vulgarity and degradation.

At the end, however, a new, more tragic, and more personal tone enters the work. After the masks have fallen and the others have left, only two characters remain: Francesca, Teresa's sister, and Moenner van der See, the only two figures who have not been bought or intimidated by the power and money of the leaders. Yet, even so, they have not been strong enough to break away and to obtain their independence. In these two people, alone, desperate, waiting for their death at the hands of the people, Adamov has gone beyond the caricature and has created a scene of tragic dimensions. Francesca and Moenner become a symbol of Western civilization which has cut itself off from the people, "a society which is going to die, its leaders more and more separated from the people, walled up in their celebrations which accustom it to death."[15] Tragic, because they are the least guilty, these two solitary individuals also share the fate of all Adamov's characters: They will die, killed by forces which they cannot control at this point in their lives. Realizing the comedy of life, recognizing its folly, they cheat their attackers by taking poison. Their suicide is a manifestation of the author's own life, and the final scene certainly indicates Adamov's attitude in this difficult period of his sickness. The freedom which the workers are seeking from their oppressors is only one part of the picture; the cry for liberty is also an anguished plea from the playwright, a plea for deliverance from his own personal torment. Thus, at the end of the play, Adamov has made a connection, although somewhat belated and perhaps even a bit tenuous, between the political and the personal situations. Yet, in this transitional work, the intrusion of the personal is forced, for Adamov had not yet succeeded in creating the balance which he was seeking. In his next few plays, he would be more successful.

IV L'Homme et l'enfant (Man and Child)

Between 1965 and 1967, Adamov went into a serious state of collapse, drinking more and more. Alcohol affected him physically and he spent much of his time in hospitals and clinics. During his long and debilitating illness, the playwright began *L'Homme et l'enfant* (*Man and Child*), a series of impressions in two parts about his past life (*Souvenirs*) and his present, tortured existence (*Journal*).

In the first part, *Souvenirs*, which occupies nearly two-thirds of the work, the dramatist offers his reflections on his childhood and adult years, as well as extensive commentaries on his theater. A semiautobiography, it is in no sense meant to be a complete recounting of his life: "No one should see in this book any faithful image of what I am. It is evident that I remembered only the most somber events; a whole aspect of my existence does not appear here. Here, there is very little amusement, very few real pleasures" (*HE*, p. 7). Adamov provides rapid, fleeting images of the events that come to his mind, recalling momentary remembrances of people and incidents. As incomplete and fragmentary as this part is, it is nevertheless the only significant published source of information on the author's life, and is also useful for an understanding and appreciation of his plays.

The second part, *Journal*, written from December, 1965, through August, 1967, is a painful account of his then-current state of physical and mental illnesses. Relating his ups and downs as he fights his disabilities, Adamov also furnishes a fascinating glimpse into his attitudes on a variety of topics, including literature and politics. During those disastrous days, he did not lose his interest in politics: Besides expressing his distress over Vietnam, he also mentions the *coup d'état* in Greece. Nor did he lose his love of literature, recalling his special appreciation of Flaubert's *L'Education sentimentale*, F. Scott Fitzgerald, and Kafka: "Why was Kafka, during such a great part of my life, the only major writer of the XXth century, the incomparable being? Why did I turn away from him? Because, in my head, all sorts of ideas changed, little by little" (*HE*, p. 243).

Principally, however, he centers upon his own weaknesses and his physical exhaustion, the idea of telephoning or even looking up a number in the directory being beyond his capabilities. His picture of himself is one of complete decay: "I feel so bad, my body wracked with sadness, teeth broken, feet turned into stone, and I am abandoned./ I have not even been asked to sign the appeal against the war in Vietnam.[16] It is not that I want to see my name in print, but the idea of not receiving a sign of life from outside . . . / What? Could I be already dead?" (*HE*, p. 207).

Throughout all of this, he finds solace in two aspects, both interrelated. One source of consolation is his wife, providing him with the necessary encouragement and help with his writing, her devotion a saving grace. The other hope comes from literature and the prospect of continuing to write. Adamov still considered the art of creation a major element in helping him to conquer his illnesses. To write, to publish, to continue seeing his plays produced will be the restoration of his life. Work becomes the salvation, the only means of avoiding the anguish which overtakes him. At one moment, he wrote: "Let me finish *M. le Modéré* [his next play] and my journal, and let me be satisfied with both of them. I need revenge" (*HE*, p. 229).

Man and Child was not meant to be a finished view of his life. The writer still looked ahead despite his pitiable state, seeing in this work a means of keeping himself alive, with his meditations on the past and present giving him the strength to continue for the future.

V *The Clown Show:* M. le Modéré (The Moderate)

When *M. le Modéré* (*The Moderate*) was published in 1968, Adamov wrote in a preliminary note to the play: *"The Moderate* is a clown's joke. I wanted it that way. . . . Surrounded by unhappiness, I either had to burst out laughing or commit suicide" (*Th.,* IV, 11). Having once developed the vein of comic, burlesque theater with *Holy Europe,* the dramatist continued along these lines, making his new work even more exaggerated and more extravagant. Like *Holy Europe, The Moderate* pictures a corrupt society in the process of decaying and rotting. The thrust of the attack this time is against the moderates, those who cannot choose, the hesitant and vacillating. Adamov detested these neutralists who always selected the safe path,[17] so unlike his own tendency toward strong, extremist positions. At the same time, however, *The Moderate* is a play of personal introspection, as the dramatist questions himself, trying to determine what brought him to the deteriorating state of his present condition.

The Moderate is a cold, harsh work. Although the dramatist never emphasized the psychological components of his characters in his previous plays, there was always some identification between character and author and character and audience. Throughout a great part of this bitter comedy (as in *Holy Europe*), there is no empathy with the characters. The figures represent various attitudes which the writer intended to mock, virtually never existing as human beings. Once more, they are puppets in a show, moving through their marionette-like paces, the strings being pulled by the cynical vision of the playwright. Moreover, Adamov had now very clearly changed the concept of the factual, historical drama which he began in *Paolo Paoli* and *Spring 71.* Obviously not in a condition to spend hours researching his work, he must have decided that he could no longer write an historical chronicle in the sense that he had originally intended, i.e., the facts and details to verify reality. The new reality would be that of a caricatural comment on life, the ridiculousness of man's existence being underlined. To avoid falling back into what he felt was the uselessness of the theater of the absurd, Adamov's caricatural comments would be very closely linked to political matters and drawn from his own storehouse of memories and experiences. In the current play and the next, *Off Limits,* the playwright centered the action not only in Paris, but in Switzerland,

England, and the United States, making use of impressions which he had received from his trips to these countries. The plays might be less specific but, perhaps, even more vitriolic.

All of this is understandable in view of the playwright's physical and emotional state at the time. Since Adamov began writing the play while he was in the hospital and later while recuperating, he could not see the world in any other way than as a terrifyingly hopeless and absurdly foolish jumble. *The Moderate* reflects completely his mood: an outer layer of sardonic humor and a strong inner core of sorrow and tragedy.

The attack is on the moderate, the neutralist ("the one whom I call that is the least moderate there is: a Centrist").[18] Adamov is trying to demonstrate that the moderate, in his insistence upon reason and logic, seeing all sides of the issues, becomes himself an immoderate, his sense of reason leading to unreasonableness, his own reality betraying reality itself. In the Prologue to the play, "M. le Modéré," called Maurice Dupré, tells the audience that he had tonsillitis as a child and he would often question his mother about the number of spots on his tonsils. Later, as an adult, he still could not stop worrying about this condition, and he constantly asked the same question of his wife, Clo, who, he reports "claimed that I asked her this question seven or eight times a day. That would have been, of course, excessive and even . . . abusive, but it wasn't true, in any case not entirely true. Actually, I asked her, I think, the previously-mentioned question five or six times a day at the most" (*Th.*, IV, 15–16). But, he continues, he could not stop questioning her because any abrupt letup would have been "exaggerated." Right away, Maurice becomes a ridiculous representative of the moderate position and, as the play unfolds, a symbol of a sick society.

Maurice is a bourgeois of Swiss background without any outstanding qualities, living in Paris with his wife, Clo, and his daughter, Mado. Clo, a little like *Mère Ubu* of Alfred Jarry's play, *Ubu roi*, is alternately commanding, imperious, fearful, and, eventually, absurd. In Adamov's stage directions, he notes that she must be both touching and grotesque at the same time, having the qualities of a person and a puppet. Mado is described as a type of "vicious schoolgirl"; totally amoral, she has a certain shamelessness about her and is inordinately interested in other people's personal lives. Clo tells Maurice that they will buy a hotel, a move which he questions, wondering if it is not a bit immoderate or excessive. As with every situation, Maurice cannot make a decision, since he must consider all aspects of the problem. Once they have talked him into buying the hotel, which has the characteristics of both a home and a bordello, the stage is set for what becomes a merciless picture of a man who represents all the weaknesses of the moderate position: He lacks solidity, decisiveness, and, from the point of view of action, he is essentially impotent. Moreover, his blind dependency on reason leads him to a justification of absurdity. In one sequence, trying to get Clo to return a key to him, he reaches a hand down her blouse, she tries to push him away, and he kicks her to the floor where she lies bleeding and yelling. Maurice tells the desk clerk of the hotel who is watching the incident with wonderment: "Don't worry about her. She raves like that almost every Wednesday. (Uneasy.) It is Wednesday today, isn't it?" Upon hearing that it is, he says, "Then, everything is in order" (*Th.*, IV, 24).

Unsure of himself, indecisive, he allows himself to be talked into all kinds of unspeakable actions: His own daughter entices him into sexual activities with herself and a female occupant of the hotel—activities which he later tries to defend with his own specious brand of reasoning. In general, even when the truth is presented to him, his sense of moderation does not allow him to accept it. Upon being told by his daughter that a singer, a tenant in the hotel, has reported seeing rats in his room, Maurice answers: "Rats, here, in our place? And . . . frequently . . . Mado, you surprise me, you surprise me greatly. If you had told me that your singer had seen, once, a mouse, I would have been able . . . if really necessary, to admit it" (*Th.*, IV, 25). Even truth, if it is excessive, cannot make its way into his concept of reality.

Maurice's inability to take a strong position and to see situations clearly because of his undue concern for moderation soon becomes his downfall. A fundamentally mediocre, petty man, he is also greedy and ambitious. Havas, an American agent, talks him into going to the "State of Jura" to head a government and to put down a revolt which is taking place. Completely unsuited to this task, Maurice accepts and is presented to his new people as their leader while he is crawling on the ground, afraid of a possible mountain avalanche, Adamov's contemptuous symbol of the leaders of the Western world. Weak and unable to cope with his situation, Maurice becomes a bully. Faced with a major strike, he decides to shoot one out of every ten strikers, after which he wonders if he has been too lenient. In this connection, the playwright makes an ironic statement on the use of power when it appears that, in fact, Maurice *was* too lenient: He is overthrown by the chief of police who knows how to use power cruelly and brutally, killing five out of every ten strikers, thus breaking the strike and solidifying his regime, a not-so-happy observation by the dramatist on the real source of authority.

In the third section of the play, Maurice, having lost his leadership, has taken refuge in London. He is now paralyzed, the paralysis serving as a symbol of the uselessness of his life and, perhaps, as a sign of retribution for his ineffective existence. He still, however, has not grasped what has happened to him. Although he is confined to a wheelchair, a virtual vegetable, like the *Mutilé* in *The Maneuver*, he calls out: "O Lord, thank you for the moderation which You have shown in my regard. When I think that You have struck only my left side, when, holding me in Your vigorous arms, it would have been so easy for You to strike my right side at the same time" (*Th.*, IV, 66). Maurice is paying for his middle-of-the-road position and, in this last part, he lives out his own personal hell.

The weaknesses of his moderation have led him to immoderate, excessive actions: Just as he was not able to turn away from Mado's sexual temptations, nor Havas' political enticements, so now he will be too weak to resist the lure of alcohol. As he proceeds inevitably into a state of total collapse, he meditates upon what went wrong and asks the Lord to give him a sign of what he should have taken into consideration as a leader—national independence? Supranational sovereignty? At this, the voice of the Lord (who shares the same opinions as Havas, the American agent, observes Adamov), thunders forth: "Europe!" In other words, Maurice did not follow the American wish that he work for a united Europe, possibly through the Common Market, thus insuring American domination. Adamov's political lesson is clear: The moderate will be shoved out of power by imperialism, particularly by American imperialism. While writing this in 1967, the Greek regime was overthrown by the military with, in Adamov's opinion, the help of the Americans (*HE*, p. 215). What is needed, says the dramatist, is force and determination; those who spend their time in excessive, paralyzing reasoning will never succeed; moderation is an infirmity.

In *The Moderate*, Adamov intended to depict the depraved and dissolute society of Western civilization. For example, the English

Prince of Wales, who marries Mado later in the play, also has a male lover on the side, making manifest that sexual depravity is found not only in the family circle, but in the government as well. When the chief of police is in the process of overthrowing Maurice's government, he blames his brutality on the fact that Mado will no longer sleep with him. And Maurice is at the center of this sexually immoral society. At one point he even has his wife dress up in the costume of the *Directoire* period,[19] a period which attracts and entices him because it was moderate—"peaceful and military, republican and authoritarian." As Margaret Dietemann notes, "His sexual aberration indicates the historical extent of his depravity. It stretches backward in time to the Directoire, which put an end to the hopes of the French Revolution, and forward in time, to the future, as he joins in the corruption of his child, who is a diseased product of his sick society."[20]

Yet, behind all the political decay, the play is also meant to express the personal decay which Adamov was experiencing at the time. Maurice's situation is very similar to Adamov's and, like the playwright, he will not be able to exist without tears. At one moment, when Mado finds Maurice weeping, she asks him what is wrong. He replies: "Everything," sobbing even more loudly. In his journal, Adamov commented on this aspect: "To write this clown play in the state in which I find myself! Of course, the clowns will cry" (*HE*, p. 226).

Nevertheless, the destruction of the central figure no longer comes from unnamable forces or even from a socioeconomic system which leaves him helpless. Rather, Maurice has been responsible for his own destiny and has failed. Not having sufficient strength of character, choosing a path that was unsuitable, he is defeated by his own decisions; lacking the ability to cope, he turns to alcohol and further deterioration. Maurice's fundamental weakness, his moderation, leads to his sexual corruption, his inability to rule, and his final decline into an alcoholic state. The parallel to Adamov's own situation at that time is, of course, striking, and we can understand that Maurice's meditations on what went wrong with his life were also those of Adamov. It is now likely that, on some level of his psyche, Adamov accepted the fact that a certain amount of the responsibility for his plight must be placed upon his own weaknesses, his own inability to survive without the help of alcohol. The play's sense of disintegration and dissolution is so strong that André Steiger, when he directed the work at the Théâtre des Mathurins on September 27, 1968, placed the action of the comedy in a hospital; Maurice wore pajamas and the clown-like music was interspersed with ambulance sirens.

While an interesting progression in the dramatist's theater, *The Moderate* seems incomplete. Even though the characters are meant to be clowns, they do not have the consistency and especially the subtlety that even cartoon-like figures can possess, nor does the play reveal the craftsmanship and concern for structure which were present in Adamov's previous works. Each scene in this work is filled with absurd situations, which are often confusing and difficult to follow. A series of short sketches, *The Moderate* lacks not only substance, but coherence. This time, Adamov's grotesque vision was too absurd for his own theater.

VI   Je . . . Ils . . . (I . . . They . . .)

Following the critical and financial success of *Man and Child*, Adamov decided to continue probing into his remembrances of his life, particularly his adolescence and young adulthood. Rereading *The Confession*, the author planned to publish the work again under the title, *Je . . . (I . . .)*, accompanied by a new series of impressions which he would write about his early life, entitled *Ils . . . (They . . .)*. The writer stated that he did not know how to define these impressions, which were most often of a sexual nature, but he added: "All I know is that these accounts are neither a series of 'short stories,' nor a collection of poems in prose. These remembrances, some real, others fictitious, are indeed memories, in any case. And, in that respect, they necessarily draw nearer to the remembrances of *The Confession*, but here I really defy anyone to find any traces of a metaphysics, only those traces of a sick childhood and adolescence."[21]

Having completed these writings in the Summer of 1968, he published them in 1969. In the more recent section, *They . . .*, Adamov hoped to complete what he had started but not finished in *The Confession*. He would be more honest, especially about his sexual feelings, he would call things directly by their names without use of euphemisms, he would no longer try to explain, justify, or excuse himself. In *They . . .*, the masculine being exists by his desperate attempt to find some sort of contact with the female, a contact which generally includes scenes of humiliation. The remembrances are composed of a succession of scenes in which the narrator, presumably Adamov or the fictitious creation of his imagination, is being put through a grotesquely masochistic torture and humiliation: He is slapped by women, usually prostitutes; he crawls on the floor toward them; they spit and step upon him. In one passage, he comments: "He told himself that he would like her to harm him. He imagined her whipping him and looking at him twisting in torture, looking at him for a long time, with her serious eyes" (*Ils . . . , * p. 233).

The stories are all similar, countless variations on the same theme and, at the center of everything, humiliation by a woman: "He had hidden nothing from her, she knew, and, in general, she joined even more with the others, with her friends, in humiliating him, making him 'incapable of harming,' as she said" (*Ils . . . ,* p. 179). Sexual degradation, fear, and sadness are once again his most vivid memories. Although the texts are direct evocations of the author's feelings of eroticism and masochism, they are also, in Adamov's own words, "images of desolation," sad commentaries on the terrible anguish of living.

VII   *The American Play:* Off Limits

From a structural and thematic point of view, *Off Limits,* composed in 1968, is one of the most ambitious works written by the dramatist. While not his best play, it is nonetheless the truest reflection of Adamov's concept of theater. *Off Limits* shows the essential oneness, the fundamental unity of his writing, in which the curable and incurable aspects are merged, and both fantasy and ideology play significant roles. Adamov was seeking a new form of theatrical reality in which the individual and social situations could be seen as equally important parts of human existence. He wanted to find a balance between the outer and inner worlds, a symbiosis between the person and society. At this moment in his career, Adamov realized that man's awareness of himself and his awareness of the world in which he lived were mutually related—in this respect, *Off Limits* is the most mature of the many Adamovian efforts.

His vision of the political state of the world is the same as that which he had already sketched out in *Holy Europe* and *The Moderate*: the declining society of Western civilization. In this case, drawing upon the memories of his visits to the United States, Adamov pays special attention to what he considers to be the total degradation of the current American society based upon alcohol, drugs, and sex. The final image of the play contains the work's political theme: the Statue of Liberty, cracked down the center, a flawed symbol of a flawed country. All of this is performed against the backdrop of the Vietnam war, which was probably the original emotional source of the writing: In Adamov's tableau, the moral decay and rot of the Vietnam situation are symptomatic of the moral decay and rot in American society.

The title itself contains both the political and personal references. "Off Limits" is a sign which Adamov saw at the entrance of the red-light district in Hamburg, Germany. The sign, placed by the American military, signified that the American soldier was no longer protected by his country if he crossed into the section; it therefore represented the forbidden.[22] At the same time, the title could refer to a personal limit beyond which people were not to go or they would be guilty of transgression, requiring some form of punishment, a curious remembrance of *The Confession* again, indicating that Adamov's fears and obsessions were still present to haunt him.

The play is not composed of scenes, but rather of "parties" and, within the "parties," a series of "happenings," which Adamov claimed he actually saw or heard about while he was in New York. Like the cartoon figures in *Holy Europe*, the characters in *Off Limits*, through their "parties" and "happenings," carve out their own versions of reality, a reality which allows them to wall themselves up within their own limited sphere. Their worlds, those of big business, industrialism, and capitalism, are hollow and empty, void of any real human relationships, a place where opportunism and exploitation are the key elements. Like the Agha in *Holy Europe*, most of the people in the play are usually inebriated: they control much of the money and, hence, the power; yet alcohol has so deadened their sensibilities that they are indifferent to the country's real needs.[23] Theirs is a counterfeit life because it does not recognize realities, particularly the realities of the Vietnam war, which becomes the leitmotif of the work. As Adamov observes: "I do not think that life can be true and possible in the 'city' as long as the nightmare of colonial war and oppression continues, without even speaking of other nightmares."[24]

The author locates his story in New York in the 1960's, centering the action around Sally and Jim, two young people of sixteen and seventeen respectively, who have fallen into what Adamov sees as the great imperialist trap of American society: Both of these desperate and impassioned people have entered the drug scene and have become addicts. They take the American society for what it is worth, realizing its commercialization, yet allowing themselves to be part of the exploitation process (Sally is a former prostitute who appears in television commercials, Jim sells his poetry to the publishing establishments). Sensing their own part in the capitalist system in which money is more important than human values, they decide to flee the country. When they are shot at the Mexican border in an almost suicidal attempt to show the world their hatred of the United States, their gesture becomes meaningless because, in their death, they are still taken over by the business enterprises of the U. S. Humphrey O'Douglas, an official of a television network, who has used the Vietnam war and turned it into a television spectacular, will now do the same thing with the story of Jim and Sally, sensationalizing it and making it a travesty of their actions.

All of this takes place in a dead society, a lifeless outgrowth of a frantic flight from reality. Interspersed throughout the "parties," the "happenings," which are meant to be improvised, spontaneous events, seem as if they have already been prepared ahead of time, as if the words are simply being repeated. These "happenings," which Adamov equated with The Living Theater of Julian Beck and Judith Malina,[25] are false because they are an avant-garde pathway leading nowhere, like a theater that closes up unto itself. Sometimes, however, when the young people take charge, the "happenings" accidentally hit upon central issues. When one of the young people asks the group, "What is reality for you?", the answers give an insight into Adamov's own vision of life at the time: "Reality is— Death." "A fiction, a dream." "A manner which is suitable for looking at the world." "The violation of the 17th parallel." "Discouragement." Finally, one character, instinctively aware of the group's situation, responds: "But there isn't any reality, there isn't any!" (*Off Limits*, pp. 71–72).

To a great extent, there is no reality for Humphrey O'Douglas and his friends, for they have succeeded in ignoring or eliminating it through alcohol, sex, drugs, or "happenings." Here, Adamov's lesson is both political and personal. His first picture is that of a declining, deteriorating society out of touch with life. At the same time (and undoubtedly Adamov was also drawing a very personal lesson), the dramatist is saying that the use of crutches like drugs or alcohol in order to avoid and obscure reality renders man impotent and unproductive. In large measure, the political and personal in this play are mutually reactive, the particular and the general have the same ending. The lesson is similar: Man who cannot cope and cannot face matters directly will be crushed, either like the cartoon figures of *Holy Europe*, "N." of *The Parody*, or Maurice of *The Moderate*.

As in all of his plays, the playwright recognizes the presence of the incurable element of life. In each one of the characters, both young and old, an impression of futility and sadness is all-pervasive. Obviously an indication of Adamov's own discouragement and overwhelming depression, this hopelessness now recalls the world of Chekhov more strongly than that of either Brecht or Strindberg. The characters reflect the despair and the aborted dreams which also mark the work of the Russian playwright. However, man can do something about his situation, life is "curable." In this context, the dramatist's sympathies go to the young, to Jim and Sally and to their friends, Bob and Peter. Although critical of their having avoided life by falling into the drug habit, Adamov nevertheless realizes that they are the only ones who have some sense of reality. The "happenings" of the young people recount the horrors of war, especially the Vietnam war; like annoying insects, they are always there, trying to penetrate the adult consciousness. In the final scenes, the young provide Adamov with hope for the future—a hope that comes from revolt, from saying "No" to the system. Peter is among the nineteen students from Yale University who have been arrested for tearing up their draft cards. Through such actions, Adamov places his confidence in posterity.

It would be nevertheless unfair to say that Adamov limits his interest only to the young: At times, there is a strong feeling of compassion for all humanity. At moments, he moves away from the satirical derision and the caricatural figures to an understanding and appreciation that all men are equally caught up in the deadening web of life. Reverting to his first phase, but to a more mature, less self-pitying version of it, Adamov recognizes man's condition, as Bernard Dort observes: "The characters are trapped in a situation which was established a long time in advance and they cannot stop playing this situation out among themselves, exhausting all the possibilities but not succeeding in getting out of it, by inventing something new, in a constant repetition which has no other exit than death, unless they are already in this very death."[26] Death, particularly death by suicide, dominates the work; inevitably it comes to the foreground, eventually equating or surpassing the harsh reality of the Vietnam war.[27] At first, one of the people hears that an acquaintance has committed suicide; next, the audience learns that Luce, one of the characters in the play, has also taken her own life; Jim and Sally die; and, finally, Humphrey O'Douglas, the powerful television tycoon, dies on stage, calling out the word, "Reality." This is Adamov's irremediable aspect of life, the reality of death which cannot be changed.

To express this intermingling of personal and social realities, the playwright had recourse to a complicated and intricate structural arrangement: "Party" sequences, "happenings," poetic interludes, and transitions constitute the framework of the play. Each of the "parties" and "happenings" provides a direct presentation of the action, as unreal as it often seems, while the poetic interludes and transitions furnish the background and interpretive comments, almost like a Greek chorus. The frenetic, feverish style, with the rapidly-changing scenes, which tended to mar the virtually dehumanized arrangement in *The Moderate*, succeeds reasonably well in this case, for the constant agitation makes an appropriate statement about the quality of life which the people are leading. Moreover, the distortion of reality which permeates the play is entirely in keeping with the characters' own perverted, twisted sense of the real. In the "parties" and "happenings," real life seems far removed from what is taking place. And, in the poetic interludes and transitions, which would presumably be the domain of the unreal, with stylized and metaphorical language, the audience is often given a more accurate interpretation of the situation.[28] Using a form of free verse, Adamov unveils the complicated drug-oriented relationship of Sally and Jim and also uses the poetic form to express his opinions on man, the Vietnam war, and death.

This was the first time that the playwright attempted to use poetry in a serious manner in his works. The form and inspiration probably came from his contacts with the "beat" poets, particularly Allen Ginsberg, when Adamov visited the United States. In fact, most of the inspiration for *Off Limits* came from the United States. In this respect, Adamov has admitted that much of what he was saying was a bit presumptuous: "It does not matter that I lived a few months in the U.S.A., I don't have full control over the events, as I would have if the play took place in France. Here, I know; there, I presume" (*Off Limits*, p. 9). Actually, the characters and incidents came from both trips which he made, first in 1959 and then in 1964. After the second visit, however, the Vietnam war helped to codify many of his ideas. In New York, the dramatist met a real Sally and Jim (not their actual names), whose adventures were similar to those presented in the play; he was introduced to them at a party at the home of a television magnate who served as one of the models for Humphrey O'Douglas. Many of the characters in the play grew out of the people whom he met at this party. James Andrews, the journalist who befriends Sally and Jim, is really an American writer named James Mills, who published the book, *The Panic in Needle Park* (New York: New American Library, 1967). This book, which describes the author's encounter with drug addicts, was also a source of considerable importance, especially in providing further details for the characterizations of Jim and Sally.[29] In addition, Adamov consulted a book on social games based upon psychological tests which helped him with the themes of the "happenings"; and he also read various collections of poetry, including those of then-new writers like Ginsberg.

Off Limits is thus a compilation of many factors: Adamov's trips to the United States, his own torment over the Vietnam war, some outside influences, and the dramatist's tremendous emotional and physical anguish of that period. At first glance, the work seems like another one of the political diatribes which the author had been writing since 1957, for Adamov is decidedly dealing with contemporary social reality, notably with the decline of American society. Nevertheless, behind the succession of "parties" and "happenings," behind the Vietnam war which was draining the U.S. in Adamov's view, there lies the certainty of death. The incurable is inseparably tied to the curable. The subject is the crisis of our society but, at the same time, this crisis is very much a part of the uncertainties and the contradictions of the human condition. The balance of the particular and the general, the individual and society which Adamov was seeking, was now found. Unstable, precarious, this balance would not last (in his next and final play, the dramatist would have already lost it). Yet, its momentary realization gives an idea of Adamov's mature, reflective concept of theater.

This vision, with its blend of reality and fantasy, political commitment and personal obsessions, was perhaps ahead of its time. The play was first presented in Aubervilliers at the Théâtre de la Commune outside of Paris on January 25, 1969, and in February of the same year at the Piccolo Teatro in Milan. Gabriel Garran, the director of the French version, feels that the work was too avant-garde at that point for public acceptance.[30] In 1969, the political situation in Vietnam had changed somewhat and the French public had temporarily lost some of its interest. Moreover, according to Garran, the musical *Hair* had not yet set the pace for a freer dramatic form, a more deliberately radical break with traditional theater. Adamov nevertheless referred to the drama as his favorite (a comment which he tended to make about the play which he was working on most recently), "my preferred play because it is the most abrupt and the one in which the thin and gentle smile of tenderness comes forth amidst all of the phantoms. My *Ping-Pong* renewed."[31] The reference to *Ping-Pong* is the fact that *Off Limits* is the first play since the 1955 work in which the playwright succeeded so well in fusing the individual and the social.

Ultimately, and this is probably one of the reasons that *Off Limits* is less successful than *Ping-Pong*, the 1969 play is meant to unsettle the spectator and leave him disoriented: "Let the spectator-listener not know where he is going to be taken, almost to the end of the play, right up to the last images which have not been understood" (*Off Limits*, p. 12). A reflection of the dramatist's illness, *Off Limits* betrays a sense of nervousness and a feeling of impatience which *Ping-Pong* does not have. And, more significantly, *Ping-Pong* is a play of strong but measured observations in which the author's opinions are expressed with controlled reflection. *Off Limits*, on the other hand, is a work of extreme opinions, the characterizations and the political comments are presented in stark black-and-white terms; the play inevitably suffers because of this.

VIII   *The Final Statement:*
Si l'été revenait (If Summer Should Return)

In 1968, Adamov began *Si l'été revenait* (*If Summer Should Return*), his most open and, paradoxically, his most secret play. Like *I . . . They . . .* , *If Summer Should Return* recalls the emotions of Adamov's childhood, adolescence, and young adulthood, in which fear, sadness, and guilt were dominant forces. The play, published in 1970 following his death, is a return to the obsessions and neuroses of the early years within the family circle and their influence upon Adamov's adult life. In addition, these obsessions, while clearly the major thrust of the work, are also associated with the political and social background, an important, but not central, part of the play. *If Summer Should Return* is the playwright's most revealing effort, touching directly upon subjects which had been only suggested before, notably upon sexual topics like incest and possibly homosexuality. Unfortunately, many of the references in the work are so personal and so allusive that much of the full impact is, of necessity, lost.

This is a play about happiness, or at least the quest for happiness. It is also a play about failure, decline, and sorrow. Adamov's recent devastating illnesses and the subsequent reflections on his life undoubtedly led to this quite intimate work, a summing up of his life and of the torments which had plagued him from childhood through his adult years. It is his final and still futile attempt to come to grips with his anguish.

Basically, Adamov is dealing with the guilt which had pursued him during his lifetime, a guilt which, in the play, is directed mainly toward the family group. At first it seems as if the playwright has made a full circle and returned to the early days of *The Parody* and *The Invasion*, because, superficially, the subject matter is the same and the obsessions are often quite similar. Nevertheless, the treatment is much more complex and, at times, subtle, and, although from the point of view of structure this is his most fantastic and dreamlike creation, the action, situated firmly in the social realities of the day and exposing openly much of the author's psyche, is far removed from the "no-man's-land" of his early writings.

This is Adamov's "Swedish play," which was the working title the dramatist gave to it before he came up with his final version. In fact, he had been very much impressed by the Swedish brand of socialism and he planned to write a work about this "ideal state." However, as he progressed in his writing, he soon turned away from a sociopolitical work to a much more personal play. The other working titles indicate his gradual change: *L'Etat providence* (*The Providence State*), a reference to Sweden; then *J'ai peur* (*I am Afraid*); and finally, *Si l'été revenait*, a more all-encompassing choice and more faithful to the theme. Since a good part of the work is a presentation of sexual aberrations, it also apparently seemed suitable to the playwright to utilize the country where sexual mores were considered freer. As he indicated in his preface, the play deals with incest "which dare not be expressed as such, even in the most modern countries. For this reason among others, it is not by chance that the play takes place in Stockholm."[32]

The play is about Lars and his personal and social relationships with the world around him. Structurally speaking, it is divided into four parts, or more specifically, the four dreams or nightmares of the leading characters: Lars, his sister Thea, his wife Brit, and a friend Alma. Each of the four dreams is a different perspective of Lars and his life. Adamov noted this: "I thought for a while that I would call this play, *Variations on the Same Theme*. But that would have precisely revealed the theme, something a title cannot allow itself, even if the play which bears it seems obscure at first glance" (*Si l'été*, p. 9). A confusing play, this work represents the most phantasmagoric atmosphere yet invented by the playwright, with a constant break in logical thought, an association of seeming non sequiturs, and a continual ambiguity in the characterizations, each person representing a variety of points of view and attitudes. Within the four different versions of the story, there is no objective truth, no hard core of reality to grasp. Continuing with the structural pattern which he had established in the second phase of his writing, Adamov uses a sort of "dream-within-a-dream" arrangement which, like the *guignols* of *Spring 71* or the flashbacks of *The Politics of Waste*, provide a deeper understanding and appreciation of the theme. The entire play is a series of dreams, but the extreme left of the performing area is used for the "latent" dreams, offering a more honest accounting of the characters' feelings.[33]

Within this nightmarish framework, the playwright's guilt is first centered on the personal relationships within the family circle. In the first three dreams, Lars expresses his guilt toward the women in his life: mother, sister, and wife. The mother figure, Mrs. Petersen, is possessive and domineering, like the previous figures in *The Invasion* and *One Against Another*, trying to invade and control her son's life until he is left with no freedom. Conveying Adamov's own wish, Lars constantly pushes his mother to the ground or hits her. Yet, the guilt feelings remain. Just as Adamov felt ashamed over the fact that his mother had died in a hospital and that he did not go to see her, so, in the play, Lars will regret that he did not allow his sister to accompany Mrs. Petersen on her works of "charity" when she was accidentally killed. The feeling about the mother, however, is almost minor compared to that which Lars expresses about his sister. The reason Thea did not accompany Mrs. Petersen was because Lars kept her near him, holding her hand tightly, caressing her hair: incest, the most secret desire of all, an obsession which threatens to destroy Lars's life. With a possessive mother, a sister for whom he has incestuous feelings, Lars's troubles are compounded: He does not succeed professionally. He tries different fields of study—architecture, botany, medicine—but fails at each of them, sometimes almost self-destructively, as the time that he slaps the Rector of the medical school, causing him to be dropped as a student. But an even greater disaster remains: He is unable to have a successful relationship with his wife, he is incapable of making her happy. Lars's difficulties, Adamov implies, are essentially sexual. In one scene, he dresses up as a little girl and bounces a child's ball on the floor prompting Mrs. Petersen to say: "How you resemble the little boy whom I loved and pressed against my bosom" (*Si l'été*, pp. 33–34). Perhaps as a result, there is also a suggestion that Lars is capable of a homosexual relationship with his friend Viktor.

In these dreams Lars calls out desperately for the ability to deal with the world and people around him as a mature and responsible adult. His failure to cope with the adult world creates tensions which are presented by means of the play's major "object," a seesaw. Lars is always on the seesaw with one or more of the women, while still another pushes it up and down, the object becoming a symbol of both fear and uncertainty (when the seesaw is set in motion) and of a desire for equilibrium, a balance in life, an equilibrium which can come only from his wife Brit, the only person whom he truly loves and the one who can save him. As he observes, "You cannot know how much I love you for not having let me continue toward my natural inclinations" (*Si l'été*, p. 61). It is she who will provide him with the strength to rid himself of his past, to accept the present moment.

Happiness will come not only from an obliteration of the memories of the early life, but from professional success as well. As Brit comments, "He will have all the necessary courage, and society will end up by recognizing him" (*Si l'été*, p. 34). Yet, this dream—similar to Adamov's own lifelong hope—is more an unfulfilled wish than an actual reality. Nothing in any of the four sequences gives the impression that Lars will actually be able to exorcise his masochistic feelings of recrimination. Even the devotion of Brit remains clouded and ambiguous, for it is Alma, a friend of both Brit and Lars, who introduced them, and it is also Alma, described by Adamov as an "androgynous beauty," who is seen embracing Brit in the latter's "latent" dream sequences, suggesting ambivalent emotions in Lars's wife.

In Alma's dream, the fourth in the group, the spectator sees that Lars's personal state, with its multiple neuroses and fears, is not that far removed from the sociopolitical situation. Michel Berto comments that "it seems that in this work Adamov succeeded in building a bridge between his two styles, that of the theater of the absurd and that of political theater, for, without any doubt, *If Summer Should Return* is also a political play, but in a more subtle and more profound manner than before."[34] Alma, the character who expresses Adamov's political and social concerns, also shares his desire for justice. Viktor tells her: "Do you know, Alma, that I am only a loan, and that at any moment the distributor of security can claim me back? They haven't fixed the date of reimbursement." To this, Alma replies: "We are all like you, all loans, and that is why I want man to be treated as a man, whatever he may be, wherever he may be. And that is indeed why I want justice to be rendered" (*Si l'été*, p. 70). Alma's comments underscore the dramatist's point of view that all men share the same human fate, death, and that while they are living, it is essential that each one have his fair share as a human being. Once again, the curable and incurable elements in human existence are recognized.

As in his previous works, Adamov lashes out at a society which he considers repressive and indifferent to the needs of mankind. Viktor spends most of his time dressed in hospital clothes, almost as if he were a prisoner of the State, probably symbolizing the feeling experienced by the playwright while in hospitals and clinics. At one moment, Viktor cries out at the director in the hospital: "For a long time, I have been noticing with fear and astonishment your aggressiveness against me. I have done nothing against the safety of the State. I have not even spoken of the indefeasible right of people to decide for themselves. In any case, you have no rights over my person, either moral or physical" (*Si l'été*, pp. 21–22). While Viktor's plight might seem like the hopelessness and frustration felt by "N." in *The Parody*, he is nonetheless very much a part of

Adamov's second phase of writing, rebelling not against unnamed forces, but against a specific source, the State. The State, or at least its representatives, are bumbling oafs, insensitive to their people (perhaps the playwright's commentary on the ten years of the de Gaulle regime). Mrs. Petersen, blissfully separated from the economic horrors of life, dresses as a clergyman and visits the miners in Kiruna[35] to perform her works of charity. While there, she reads from the Bible, insulting the impoverished, hopeless miners with stories of precious jewels and expensive stones, an example of the cruel and needless indifference of those in power.

There is, however, one major change in this, Adamov's final, play. The type of frontal assault on society made by the playwright in *Holy Europe*, *The Moderate*, or *Off Limits* has been lessened to a great extent. At this juncture in his life, the dramatist appears to have lost some of the faith which he once placed in the efficacy of social and political action; if Alma is to be taken as an example, the dramatist may have had serious doubts about the validity of his own political commitment. Alma is often ridiculed by the other characters for her sociopolitical activities and, at one point, Thea mentions that Alma gives a tremendous amount of herself in her work to help humanity not so much to aid others as to make herself important in their eyes. In his own comments about her, Adamov noted: "Poor Alma, victim of her own pseudosuperiority, who will go off to the third world and will recognize that she cannot resolve any problem there, and will kill herself because of that also, without counting the personal reasons, of course" (*Si l'été*, p. 10). It soon becomes apparent that Alma's political interests may be closely tied to her sexual obsessions and that her involvement with the third world may simply be an outlet for sexual frustration. Alma and her situation are also perhaps an indication that Adamov now felt that the political realm could be equally as deceptive and disillusioning as the personal.

As the title indicates, the play is a wish for a return to the innocence and happiness which summer can bring, perhaps a former summer unknown to Adamov, unclouded by failure, guilt, and recrimination. In the context of Adamov's disillusionment, however, if there is any possibility of such a happiness, it can be achieved only through deliberate self-deception. In the final scene of the play, Lars and Brit are alone together on the seesaw, Mrs. Petersen is asleep, and Alma and Thea have fallen to the floor. Lars kisses Brit and says: "Finally, everything is settled!" indicating that all his obsessions have been conquered and that he can live in peace with his wife. In this last moment, Adamov's point is clear: Lars is deluding himself—his obsessions, both personal and even political, are still present and his respite is only temporary. In this nightmarish world, he will soon be caught up again in his neuroses. Life itself is an immense farce and a deep torment. In this respect, at least, the last comment made by the playwright is one of sadness and pessimism. Nonetheless, Adamov's final play is a fairly direct accounting of his situation, containing a lucid, mature realization of man's fate. To that extent, it represents the only victory which the dramatist can hope for in coping with reality.[36]

Although Adamov was now physically debilitated, he did not look upon *If Summer Should Return* as his final word. At the time of his death, he was in the process of preparing a work on Ferdinand de Lesseps, who was involved in the construction of the Suez and Panama Canals. The playwright apparently conceived of this work as a huge, allegorical piece in which the characters would be gigantic creations, such as the Mediterranean and Red Seas, the Pacific and Atlantic Oceans. Fragments from this last effort have been published in René Gaudy's study (pp. 162–63) and Pierre Mélèse's work (pp. 136–48).

CHAPTER 5

Conclusion

IN the final analysis, Adamov's writing is a desperate attempt to relate to the world around him, to find a way of adjusting to the nightmare of living. The dramatist himself is the subject of his plays, and every one of his works, whether a part of his personal theater or of his political commitment, is a representation of the deep and vital concerns of the playwright. Looked at in their totality, his plays are an extraordinary account of a man and his alienation and separation, for, basically, this is a theater of separation. Uprooted from his birthplace, Adamov spent his life as a foreigner, both physically and psychically, experiencing anomie and the absurdity of living. Isolated, alone with his torments, the writer reached out for an elusive contact, not simply with the universe in which he had been placed, but with the people who surrounded him and the socio-economic systems in which they functioned. In all of this, he was seeking what the dream recreated in *Professor Taranne* had told him: his own sense of identity.

Adamov's personal struggle was painful and, inevitably, unsuccessful, for he never managed to deal with the world on its own terms. It is not by accident that his plays became a reflection of this torture and it is not by accident that almost all of the works (even the political pieces) are, in one form or another, dream plays, which come from the world of nightmares, the real world of the dramatist. In all of his writings, the characters are people who have lost or are about to lose the battle with life. In this mélange of masochism, remorse, frustration, and hostility, Adamov's figures continually experience one sentiment: fear, especially fear of death. From his first play to his last, his characters are confronted with and surrounded by death. At times, as in the case of "N," this becomes a sign of the futility and hopelessness of living and simply the final destruction of a life that has already been destroyed. At other moments, it is a means of escape, as in Pierre's suicide or Sally's and Jim's willful death. Death can also be brought about by man's inhumanity to his fellowman as in *Spring 71*. In the overall context, it is evident that the "incurable" aspect of life is always at the basis of each one of Adamov's plays. While the "curable" side of existence provided him with a temporary diversion or a sort of life raft to which to cling, the playwright never forgot his primary image of the helplessness of man adrift in the universe.

I   The Dramatist's Progression

In spite of these hopeless "givens" which permeate his writing, his work can be said to have a sort of progression (although it is somewhat difficult to talk about a progression when dealing with plays that are so closely connected to the complex personality of an individual). Nevertheless, we can see a pattern in Adamov's writings in which he struggled to cope with life, attempted to achieve a sense of maturity. Throughout all of his theater and during his lifetime, the author was really expressing a feeling of injustice at the way that life had treated him and, at all times, there is a sense of persecution, a feeling of being victimized by something or by someone, a paranoid reaction to the world, its people, and its systems. All of his plays deal with justice or injustice in one form or another, accompanied by masochistic guilt feelings as well as a desire to blame others. The real development can be seen in the manner in which Adamov handled these feelings and, in that respect, came to limited terms with reality.

In the first plays, the dramatist was concerned with the nameless, frightening forces which prevented him from functioning as a human being. Sometimes these forces came from an indifferent fate, with everybody sharing the same final destiny, death. Other times, as in *The Maneuver*, fate turned out to be man's own psyche, his obsessions and neuroses having taken control. In *Professor Taranne*, his best play in this early period, Adamov continued to explore this theme: man as the victim of unknown opponents, either within himself or within the universe. Eventually, he tried to trace the responsibility to more specific sources. At first, he placed the blame on the family: Father, mother, sister all share the responsibility. It was probably necessary that he put some of the burden on their shoulders, if only to alleviate the terrible guilt feelings which he felt toward all three. As we know from his personal life and from comments made in *As We Were*, the father represents the dramatist's failure to meet the expectations of another human being and, in spite of the father's weaknesses and lack of interest in the family, the dramatist felt guilty over his death. The mother plays an even more direct role, a symbol of the oppressive, overwhelming force in the lives of the protagonists in the plays, rendering them weak, debilitated, and impotent. As in the case of the father, there is also a feeling of duty not performed on Adamov's part and, hence, guilt. However, the son figures in the plays rebel against the domineering, intrusive presence of the mother and, at times, even react against this authority in a physical way, kicking, pushing, or shoving the mother to the ground. Probably more than any other character, the mother becomes the source of the son's inability to function in an adult world, of his difficulty in developing a mature relationship with another person, particularly a female. Finally, the Adamov "heroes" reveal an even greater sense of guilt toward the sister, who, like the protagonists in the plays, is one of life's victims, never able to obtain what she wants or needs, never able to function within the normal codes of society. With the father, mother, and sister figures, the Adamov hero alternates between an almost incapacitating sense of guilt and a rejection of this burden placed upon him, moving from a masochistic acceptance of recrimination to a rebellion against the people responsible.

A similar ambivalent, love-hate relationship applies as well to the playwright's treatment of women. In *The Parody*, the writer established his concept of the eternal female: faithless, flitting from one man to another, cruel, indifferent. Later, in *The Maneuver*, the woman becomes as emasculating as the mother, rendering the man helpless and ineffective, inevitably having her share of the responsibility for the central character's incapacity to deal with the adult, mature world. At the same time, however, woman is also the source of most of his hope for the future. While Pierre in *The Invasion* recognizes that Agnès brings disorder and chaos into his life, he also realizes that she is the basis of his creativity and that a relationship with her is the only means at his disposal to a reasonable, sane acceptance of life. In *If Summer Should Return*, Adamov still questions the role of woman, even ascribing a lesbian aspect to her, but he nevertheless suggests that it is woman's support which will help him to survive, to be able to continue. In the final analysis, marriage with a woman (in the sense of a physical consummation of the union) will do much to achieve this long-desired stability. Apparently, from Adamov's own testimony, such an achievement was not possible for him.

If his theater is any indication, Adamov did find a period in his life when his personal neuroses were under some sort of control, thereby allowing him to turn his attention to another area of interest —the political and socioeconomic systems of the capitalist enterprise. In effect, however, this new phase was really only a logical extension of the feeling of injustice and persecution which was at the base of all of his works. This time he directed it against the capitalist system. Previously, the personal introspective obsessions had been too strong to allow the dramatist's indignation at society to emerge, although his anger had always been bubbling under the surface: The militant in *The Maneuver*, Henri in *The Direction of the March*, and Jean in *One Against Another* were all harbingers of these future concerns. *Paolo Paoli* and *Spring 71* were strongly and clearly political plays, expressing the author's outrage over social injustices, and indicating his concern for his fellow human beings, notably those of the working class. Curiously, in spite of his proclaimed affection for the workers and his intent to write for them, many of his succeeding plays had little to do with the laboring class, since the dramas were situated in a bourgeois, middle-class atmosphere.

In this second phase of his writing, Adamov had evidently come to more rational terms with himself. The somewhat irritating plaint of the victim had disapperared, but had been replaced with a didactic, strident voice. Now man could find a measure of hope in taking action, committing himself, solving the "curable" problems of life; he was no longer totally the helpless plaything of fate. At the same time, the dramatist was acutely aware that his theater could not ignore life's "incurable" matters. In *The Politics of Waste*, he began to forge a link between the individual's obsessions and society's neuroses. It was this attempt that led him into his third phase in which he tried to find a balance between the realm of the neurosis and the structure of the world in which one lives, the merger of the personal and the political.

At this point, the playwright suffered a major setback in his physical condition, seriously marking his work. Ill a great deal of the time, he was often unable to write and there was a long hiatus between works. The plays now possessed a nervous, restless, almost uncontrollable quality, on the one hand a result of the playwright's attempts to make a more imaginative use of the stage, on the other a reflection of his own mental and physical deterioration. It would have been nice to report that the theater played a significant role in allowing Adamov to come to rational terms with his life, liberating him from his neuroses, but such does not seem to be the case. Even in his final play, the neuroses are still painfully present. At this point, the dramatist left the impression that political commitment did not hold the same attraction for him, with the strong suggestion that political activity was simply a sublimation of the sexual drive and that the frustrations and anguish would continue for the Adamovian character, as well as for the dramatist himself. Yet, the playwright's last few works, particularly *If Summer Should Return*, contain a much greater honesty and directness, a more mature understanding of life, and a deeper realization of oneself and the world in which one lives. If Adamov's long quest for stability did not succeed, it did at least provide him with the only sort of triumph he could obtain, an intelligent awareness of his own existence and at least a partial fulfillment of the demands of his subconscious.

II   *The Man of the Theater*

The playwright's personal situation and its expression are the most important aspects of Adamov's theater, but not the only part worthy of consideration. His theater is also an innovative, inventive use of the stage and, while not totally successful in this respect, it is nonetheless a fascinating experiment in drama. If the term "theater of the absurd" can apply to the dramatist at all, it is most appropriately used in referring to his bold use of the acting area. Right from the outset, the conventional and traditional form of the play could not satisfy the often quixotic and bizarre vision of the writer. Like Artaud, Adamov held the view that the stage was a treasure house of unique interrelationships between dialogue, mime, setting, lighting, music. The stage was to be a visual, concrete representation of the theme to be expressed. "N.," lying prone on the floor, can suggest his real situation more clearly than words in this case; the step-by-step mutilation of the *Mutilé* conveys more stunningly than dialogue the frightening disintegration which the playwright wanted to express; the physical disorder in Pierre's house is a vivid realization of the disorder in his inner being. Objects also assumed a vital importance: The preeminence of the mother's chair in *The Invasion* powerfully emphasizes her control over her son; the woman's bicycle in *The Reunions* expresses clearly the protagonist's inability to function as a man; the seesaw in *If Summer Should Return* is a vivid example of the desire for balance and equilibrium; and the pinball machine in *Ping-Pong* becomes a major symbol of man's foolishness and wastefulness.

Most of Adamov's plays lack the normal plot structure. From the sketchy, schematic arrangement of *The Parody* to the nightmarish mosaic of *If Summer Should Return*, the dramatist never adopted the conventions of the well-made play. Most often, in addition, Adamov presented no solution to the problems posed in the plays because there was none in his own life. As he continued writing, especially at the beginning of the second phase when he began to fall under the influence of the ideas of Brecht, he became more interested in achieving a "distancing" effect via the projections in *Paolo Paoli* or the *guignols* in *Spring 71*, supplying historical background while reminding the audience that it was watching a play, keeping it emotionally separated. At the same time, he also tended to adopt a Pirandellian technique of a "play-within-a-play": in *The Politics of Waste*, flashbacks recount the background to the trial scene; in *Holy Europe* and *If Summer Should Return*, dreams within the action reveal the latent feelings of the characters; in *Off Limits*, "happenings" and poetic inserts provide further insights into the characters' relationships. At times, however, Adamov became so interested in technique that he made his works all but unperformable. This was particularly true of the later plays which became a reflection of his own worsening physical condition. The scenes pass so rapidly and with such limited development that the audience does not have time to grasp what is taking place; the effect simply leaves the spectator bewildered.

Amidst all this, Adamov did not forget the importance of dialogue. It is often thought that, like Artaud, Adamov preferred to ignore the text or relegate it to a decidedly secondary role. Careful examination of the plays reveals that this is not so. Roger Blin, who directed Adamov's first play, comments on this aspect: "Adamov believed in the text. The spectacle interested him, but as a function of the text. The spectacle was designed to aid in the comprehension of the text and to keep its mystery."[1] Language was always an important, often major, element in his writings. He never adopted the nonsequitur quality of the theater of Ionesco, for example. In general, his dialogue follows its own inner, but always understandable, logic. Adamov did, however, attempt numerous experiments with language. In *The Invasion*, he thought that he had developed a new technique when he used indirect dialogue, the characters expressing one idea but really meaning another, only to discover that Chekhov had already preceded him. In *Ping-Pong*, language was to be played against the action in order to obtain the full value of the pomposity and artificiality of the characters. In *Holy Europe* and *Off Limits*, the language varied according to the effect desired, at times involving doggerel verse to express the playwright's contempt and, at other times, approaching a freer, more liberated form of poetry to convey the depths of the soul. No one style dominates, and each individual play has its own particular expression of the author's obsessions. Within all of this, there is an undeniable absurdity, incongruity, and iconoclasm. It would be very difficult, however, to view Adamov's theater as truly humorous or comical; what might pass for humor comes out of the illogical situations and the exaggerated actions. Even in his more "comical" plays, there is too much bitterness, too much hatred. Adamov's satire, which does indeed exist, is too strong to provoke much laughter; it demands reflection and ultimately provokes sadness.

III *Adamov's Position in the French Theater*

What, finally, is Adamov's position in the French theater of the twentieth century? It is now clear that he does not rank with Ionesco or Beckett, with whom he was closely associated when all three were at the beginning of their careers. Given the totality of his work, he never achieved the heights of the two previously-named dramatists. It is also obvious that he does not fall under the rubric of the theater of the absurd, just as most playwrights cannot be so neatly categorized. His influences were many: Strindberg, Kafka, Artaud, Brecht, O'Casey, Chekhov, and possibly Pirandello, all related to his complex and varied personality.

The key to the strengths and weaknesses of the author's writing lies in his personality, for rarely has any theater been so closely attached to the psyche of the individual. Since Adamov's plays cannot really exist without an understanding of the dramatist, they are consequently often too hermetic to be appreciated, too secretive to be understood. It is probably this quality which requires us to place the dramatist into the ranks of the important, but secondary writers in French literature. Adamov generally did not succeed in taking the step that would move him from the personal to the universal; when he did turn to the world around him, as in *Paolo*

Paoli or *Spring 71*, he became unnecessarily limited in perspective, partial in view, and strident in tone. Later, when he attempted to combine neuroses and social comment, the potential was present for a truly unique theatrical expression—an expression never realized in a cohesive, fully-developed vision. Once again, Adamov's state of mind intervened, preventing him from making contact. It is unfortunately true that the contact with human beings, sought so desperately by the playwright during his lifetime, could not be found through his theater: The strange, oblique personality of the dramatist apparently did not find its proper outlet on the stage.

Nevertheless, while Adamov will never achieve the ranks of the outstanding writers, he will remain a significant and important figure of his period. Some of his works will stand up relatively well: *The Invasion* is an effective cry of anguish; *One Against Another* is a vivid expression of persecution; and *Paolo Paoli, Spring 71, Off Limits,* and *Holy Europe* all contain powerful scenes which, for one reason or another, do not sustain that power in their totality. However, it seems likely that two plays by Adamov will stand the test of time: *Ping-Pong* and *Professor Taranne*. The former achieves that difficult balance which the dramatist pursued. It is a careful blend of the personal foolishness of man linked with discreet comments on the oppressive nature of the social system. The connection of the personal and the public is well formulated in the work, the point is subtly made, and the stage becomes a concrete image of man and his folly. *Professor Taranne* is a truly fine realization of the nightmare and anguish of living. Perhaps because it is a transcription of a dream, the play has ironically a terrifying reality, a reality which comes from the truths of the subconscious. Man's quest for his identity, the confused torment of existence, and man's eventual submission and defeat are made compelling and valid. It is not by chance that both of these works achieve their effectiveness from a carefully-controlled and somewhat restrained expression of theme and structure. The hermeticism and exaggerations which mar the other plays are thankfully nonexistent and, in these two works, Adamov shows the power of his writing.

Curiously, though, the most telling work may very well have been his first, *The Confession*, the haunting reflections about his life. This revealing work may possibly outlast his theater. In spite of his many innovative theatrical techniques, Adamov never seemed entirely comfortable with the restrictions which the dramatic form imposed. The journal, with its individualistic, less restrictive style of writing, seems to have been more suitable for him. In this highly personal form, he was often able to achieve the universality that he rarely attained in his theater.

Notes and References

Chapter One

1. A part of the Russian Soviet Federated Socialist Republic, the largest and most important of the fifteen union republics that make up the USSR.

2. Pierre Mélèse, *Arthur Adamov* (Paris: Théâtre de tous les temps, 1973), p. 6.

3. Arthur Adamov, *L'Homme et l'enfant* (Paris: Gallimard, 1968), p. 15. This autobiographical work by the author will be discussed in a later chapter. Since numerous references from the book will be made throughout this study, they will hereafter be incorporated into the body of the text and referred to by the abbreviation, *HE*.

4. Martin Esslin, *The Theatre of the Absurd,* rev. ed. (New York: Anchor Books, 1969), p. 67. Since references are made to two Esslin works in this study, this particular work will be identified in the future as *Absurd*.

5. Georges Pitoëff (1886–1939) was a Russian-born actor and director active in French theater. From 1916 until his death, he and his wife, Ludmilla, presented a varied list of classic and modern plays in their repertory company, both in Geneva and in Paris.

6. Adamov also had brief contact with Paul Eluard, to whom he sent some of his poetry, and with a group of writers connected with the Surrealist movement.

7. Arthur Adamov, *Je. . . Ils. . .* (Paris: Gallimard, 1969), p. 76. The first part of this work, entitled *Je. . .,* is a reprint of *L'Aveu,* originally published by Adamov with the Sagittaire Press in 1946. All future references from *Je. . . Ils. . .* dealing with *L'Aveu* will hereafter be referred to as *L'Aveu* and incorporated into the text.

8. René Gaudy, *Arthur Adamov* (Paris: Théâtre Ouvert, 1971), p. 18.

9. Esslin, *Absurd,* p. 67.

10. Adamov was also deeply affected by the deaths of two of his closest friends, Gilbert-Lecomte and Artaud. When Adamov returned to Paris after his liberation from the prison camp, he found Gilbert-Lecomte in pitiful shape, mainly because of his dependence on drugs. Adamov remained with him through his final days. At the same time, Adamov and Marthe Robert helped free Artaud from the asylum at Rodez and stayed close to him until his death in 1948.

11. Arthur Adamov, *Théâtre II* (Paris: Gallimard, 1955), p. 8. Four

volumes of Adamov's plays have been grouped together under the title *Théatre*. Hereafter, references to any one of the four volumes will be incorporated into the text of this study and referred to by the abbreviation *Th.* and the indication of the volume number.

12. Gaudy, p. 28.

13. Preface to *La Parodie* and *L'Invasion* (Paris: Charlot, 1950), p. 16. As cited in Esslin, *Absurd,* p. 77.

14. *Ibid.*

15. Only *En Fiacre* has been published *(L'Avant-Scène,* No. 294, September 1, 1963, pp. 39–46). However, for a detailed summary of these radio plays, consult Mélèse, pp. 119–26. For a complete listing of all of Adamov's radio adaptations, see Mélèse, pp. 185–88.

16. Mélèse, p. 148.

Chapter Two

1. Esslin, *Absurd,* p. 67.

2. It is through dreams that man can understand the universe, he adds: "But nowhere more than in the dream of sleep, in the great hollow space behind our nights, does the world reveal more visibly its soul, i.e., what animates it, its movement" *(L'Aveu,* pp. 34–35).

3. The writer mentions suicide, but finds that this is not possible, not because of any instinct of self-preservation, but simply because such an act would be too monumental in view of the fact that his whole life has been marked by a strong lethargy in even the minutest matters.

4. Guillaume Apollinaire, *The Breasts of Tirésias,* trans. Louis Simpson, in *Modern French Theatre,* eds. Michael Benedikt and George E. Wellwarth (New York: E.P. Dutton, 1964), p. 66.

5. Arthur Adamov, *August Strindberg, dramaturge* (Paris: L'Arche, 1955), p. 47.

6. *Histoire du "nouveau théatre"* (Paris: Gallimard, 1966), p. 68.

7. As a result, Adamov's plays read less well than they perform.

8. Gaudy, p. 29.

9. *Ibid.,* p. 32.

10. Serreau, p. 71.

11. "Arthur Adamov and Invaded Man," *Modern Drama,* 7 (1965), 402.

12. *Eléments,* No. 1 (January 1, 1951), 25–39. The material for the discussion of *Le Désordre* comes from Mélèse's book and from a personal letter by Professor David Bradby of The University of Kent at Canterbury who has written a thesis on Adamov.

13. "The Happiest of Women" reappears in *Les Retrouvailles,* written in 1955.

14. Mélèse, p. 24.

15. Gaudy, p. 51.

16. Carlos Lynes, Jr., "Adamov or 'le sens littéral' in the Theatre," *Yale French Studies*, No. 14 (1954–1955), 52.

17. *Absurd*, p. 79.

18. Arthur Adamov, *Ici et maintenant* (Paris: Gallimard, 1964), p. 14.

19. *Ibid.*

20. The title could have several interpretations. Besides "direction," *sens* could also be translated as "meaning." And *marche* could signify "walking" or some other form of movement.

21. The play was later presented at the Théâtre de l'Oeuvre in Paris in May, 1954, along with *Comme nous avons été* under the direction of Jacques Mauclair.

22. Mélèse notes (p. 33) that the letter from the Rector was a transformation of a real-life incident involving the Belgian playwright Michel de Ghelderode. Adamov had sent Ghelderode a copy of *The Parody* and *The Invasion*, but had never received a reply. He took this silence for disapproval and the incident reappeared in his dream in the form of the Rector's letter.

23. The theme of plagiarism was not present in the original dream, but was added later by the playwright during the composition of the work (*HE*, p. 101).

24. Lynes, p. 53.

25. "Arthur Adamov et le sense du fétichisme," *Cahiers de la Compagnie Madeleine Renaud—Jean-Louis Barrault*, Nos. 22–23 (May, 1958), 184.

26. As is customary in Adamov's theater, the periods following the sentences indicate the frightening uncertainty experienced by the character; this same hesitancy was displayed by the playwright himself when he spoke.

27. Guy Verdot, *"Tous contre tous," Franc Tireur*, April 21, 1953.

28. *"Tous contre tous," Les Nouvelles Littéraires*, April 23, 1953.

29. Serreau, p. 73.

30. *The Theater of Protest and Paradox* (New York: N.Y.U. Press, 1964), p. 30.

31. *Absurd*, p. 84.

32. Serreau, p. 74.

33. Mélèse indicates that the play was written much earlier, following *The Maneuver* (p. 30).

34. Arthur Adamov, *"Comme nous avons été," La Nouvelle Nouvelle Revue Française*, 1 (1953), 435. All future references will be listed as *NNRF* and incorporated into the text.

35. Adamov later disapproved of this use of detail as a substitute for realism, calling it "one of those false concrete details which only sidetrack one" (*Th.*, II, 15).

36. Maurice Gravier, a professor at the *Faculté des Lettres* in Paris,

is the author of a major study on Strindberg, *Strindberg et le théâtre moderne* (1949).

37. *August Strindberg, dramaturge,* p. 8. Bibliographical details are supplied in Chapter 2, Note 5. All future references will be incorporated into the text and listed as *Strindberg.*

Chapter Three

1. This apparent resolution of his difficulties would not last long. In his final phase of writing, the neuroses would reappear and once again become a major part of his theater.

2. "Qui êtes-vous Arthur Adamov?" *Cité Panorama* (Program Bulletin of Planchon's Théâtre de la Cité), Villeurbanne, No. 9, 1960. As cited in Esslin, *Absurd,* p. 94.

3. Esslin calls it "one of the masterpieces of the Theatre of the Absurd" (p. 86), and Serreau also views the work as Adamov's supreme accomplishment (p. 82).

4. Serreau, p. 75.

5. Arthur is Adamov himself and Victor is the name of his close childhood friend.

6. Jean Carlier, "Adamov apporte deux billards électriques: un pour les acteurs, un pour le public," *Combat,* February 3, 1955.

7. Arthur and Victor also bring to mind the wasted lives of Frédéric and Deslauriers in Flaubert's *L'Education sentimentale.*

8. At the same time, however, Arthur does not share the total defeat experienced by the others, probably because he is the only character in the play who is interested in the machine for its imaginative aspects.

9. *Mythologies* (Paris: Editions du Seuil, 1957), p. 100.

10. *Absurd,* p. 88.

11. *Ibid.*

12. This play is *Paolo Paoli.*

13. Gaudy, p. 59.

14. Arthur Adamov, "'Woyzeck' ou la fatalité mise en cause," *Les Lettres Françaises,* November 28, 1963. As cited in *Ici et maintenant,* pp. 238–39.

15. Walter H. Sokel, ed., *An Anthology of German Expressionist Drama* (New York: Anchor Books, 1963), p. xiv.

16. *Ibid.,* pp. ix-x.

17. *Ibid.,* p. xxi.

18. This part of the theory was not entirely followed by Adamov who often allowed some audience identification with his characters. In fact, Brecht himself was not completely successful in living up to this point.

19. "Brecht's Dramatic Theory," trans. J. F. Sammons, *Merkur,* 15

(1961), 520–31. As reprinted in *Brecht (Twentieth Century Views)*, ed. Peter Demetz (Englewood Cliffs, N. J.: Prentice-Hall, 1962), p. 109.

20. Martin Esslin, *Brecht: The Man and his Work*, rev. ed. (Garden City, N.Y.: Anchor Books, 1971), p. 133.

21. *Essential Works of Marxism*, ed. Arthur P. Mendel (New York: Bantam Books, 1965), p. 6.

22. Arthur Adamov, "Théâtre, argent et politique," *Théâtre Populaire*, March 1, 1956. As reprinted in *Ici et maintenant*, pp. 30–45.

23. *Ibid.*, p. 31.

24. *Ibid.*, p. 41.

25. Claude Olivier, "'Paolo Paoli,' c'est la demi-conscience," *Les Lettres Françaises*, January 16, 1958. As cited in *Ici et maintenant*, p. 52.

26. The capital of French Guiana.

27. "Le théâtre peut-il aborder l'actualité politique?" *France-Observateur*, No. 405, February 13, 1958. As cited in *Ici et maintenant*, p. 70.

28. "Quand les critiques sont dans la pièce . . . ," *La Nouvelle Critique*, No. 94, March, 1958. As cited in *Ici et maintenant*, p. 87.

29. The title and name of the central character, Paolo Paoli, came from a play which Adamov had written a few years earlier and had then destroyed (Mélèse, p. 56).

30. The portrait of the priest is so vehement that Adamov later felt obliged to state that he considered the characterization of the abbot suitable and that the anticlerical tone of the work was not excessive.

31. "A propos de 'Paolo Paoli,'" *Théâtre Populaire*, January, 1958. As cited in *Ici et maintenant*, p. 60.

32. The actions of the characters in *One Against Another* are too suspect to be listed as "noble."

33. "Courtes remarques sur la mise en scène de 'Paolo Paoli,'" *Paolo Paoli* (Paris: Gallimard, 1960). As cited in *Ici et maintenant*, p. 96.

34. "Les papillons du bagne," *Les Lettres Françaises*, March 21, 1957. As cited in *Ici et maintenant*, p. 48.

35. Claude Sarraute, "Arthur Adamov définit un nouvel art poétique," *Le Monde*, January 19, 1958.

36. *Confédération Générale du Travail*, the workers' union.

37. *Front de Libération Nationale*, the most vociferous of groups calling for Algerian independence.

38. Arthur Adamov, *Anthologie de la Commune* (Paris: Editions Sociales, 1959), p. 11.

39. "J'aime le réel mêlé à l'irréel dans 'Les Ames mortes,' " *L'Humanité*, April 22, 1960. As cited in *Ici et maintenant*, p. 117.

40. Arthur Adamov, *Théâtre de Société* (Paris: Les Editeurs Français Réunis, 1958), p. 9.

41. The French in Algiers demonstrated on May 13, leading to a crisis in France which ended with de Gaulle's assumption of power.

42. Arthur Adamov, *"Les Apolitiques,"* *La Nouvelle Critique*, No. 101 (December, 1958), 124.

43. At the end of the Franco-Prussian war in 1871, the Parisians objected to the humiliating peace agreement with Prussia and were opposed to the national government headed by Adolphe Thiers. After failing to disarm the Parisian national guard, Thiers fled to Versailles in March, 1871, and the Parisians set up a communal government.

44. "On demande un nouveau théâtre," *The Observer*, 1962. As cited in *Ici et maintenant*, p. 131. Adamov was apparently referring to the French control of Madagascar in the postwar period until 1958.

45. "Ma 'métamorphose,'" *France-Observateur*, April 25, 1963. As cited in *Ici et maintenant*, p. 145.

46. Serreau, p. 79.

47. "A propos du 'Printemps 71,'" *La Nouvelle Critique*, February, 1961. As cited in *Ici et maintenant*, p. 119.

48. "On demande un nouveau théâtre," *Ici et maintenant*, pp. 130–31.

49. "Avec 'Le Printemps 71,' Adamov aborde l'histoire de front," *Libération*, March 19, 1962.

50. The playwright noted the connection with Brecht's *Saint Joan of the Stockyards* in which the meat-packers of the Chicago stockyards talk in the bombastic blank verse of Schiller's romantic heroes ("Lettre à Otto Haas sur la mise en scène du 'Printemps 71,'" *Les Lettres Françaises*, September 28, 1962; as cited in *Ici et maintenant*, p. 134).

51. *Ibid.*, p. 135.

52. "Quelques mots encore sur la représentation du 'Printemps 71' au Théâtre Gérard-Philipe de Saint-Denis," November, 1963. As cited in *Ici et maintenant*, p. 148.

53. Pierre Joseph Proudhon (1809–1865), French social theorist. Proudhon envisioned a social revolution which would safeguard the equality of individuals and their liberty.

54. Louis August Blanqui (1805–1881), a French revolutionist and radical thinker who had a strong influence on the Commune. He was arrested by Thiers shortly before the proclamation of the Commune.

55. "Departure from the Absurd: Adamov's Last Plays," *Yale French Studies*, No. 46 (1971), 52.

56. "Quelques mots encores," *Ici et maintenant*, p. 147.

Chapter Four

1. "On demande un nouveau théâtre," *Ici et maintenant*, p. 131.

2. Emile Copfermann, "Adamov ou le retour," *Les Lettres Françaises*, No. 1205 (October 25–31, 1967), 20.

3. "De quelques faits," *Théatre Populaire*, No. 45. As cited in *Ici et maintenant*, pp. 154–55.

4. This incident appears in *Off Limits,* another work which has the United States as a source of inspiration.

5. Once again the dramatist saw his play performed first outside of France; the work was performed in London at the Unity Theater in 1963, then at Leipzig in 1965, and in Genoa in 1966. Eventually the play was directed by José Valverde and produced at the Théâtre Gérard Philipe in Saint-Denis in October, 1967. Valverde used scenes of poverty in Newark, New Jersey, and South Africa as background to the action.

6. "Pour finir," *Ici et maintenant,* p. 171.

7. *Ici et maintenant,* p. 240.

8. Gaudy, p. 80.

9. "Pour finir," p. 177.

10. Charlemagne (Charles the Great or Charles I), 742–814, Emperor of the West and Frankish King; legend has pictured him as the champion of Christendom. Charles V (Charles the Wise), 1337–1380, King of France, 1364–1380; an able ruler, but his love of pomp and lack of economy put a severe burden on his country.

11. "Pour finir," p. 178.

12. In the dream, Adamov also makes it clear that the Pope, Innocent XXV, wishes to have nothing to do with the Christ figure; when the latter appears, the Pope goes out of his way to avoid him.

13. In most of Adamov's plays, the major themes are suggested in the first few pages.

14. Dietemann, p. 57.

15. Gaudy, p. 83.

16. In a footnote, Adamov observed that he was later asked to sign the appeal (*HE*, p. 207).

17. Gaudy comments that Adamov particularly detested neutralist countries or organizations like Switzerland and the United Nations (p. 87).

18. Copfermann, p. 20.

19. The Directory government ruled in France from 1795 until 1799, when it was overthrown by Napoléon Bonaparte.

20. Dietemann, p. 58.

21. *Je. . . Ils. . . ,* p. 163. As was previously mentioned (see Chapter 1, Note 7), *Je. . . Ils. . .* is composed of two parts; *Je. . . ,* a reprint of *L'Aveu;* and *Ils. . . ,* more recent comments on the human condition. All future references from *Ils. . .* will be incorporated into the text.

22. Gaudy, p. 96.

23. In these two recent works, alcoholism is a prominent factor and is obviously a reflection of Adamov's personal concerns.

24. *Off Limits* (Paris: Gallimard, 1969), p. 11. All future references will be listed as *Off Limits* and incorporated into the text.

25. Julian Beck and Judith Malina are part of an American avant-garde theatrical group called "The Living Theater," which has toured extensively in Europe.

26. Gaudy, p. 124.

27. In Adamov's view, the Vietnam war is simply a more gruesome, more unnecessary indication of the fate of all men.

28. The poetic passages were apparently inspired by the structural arrangement in Eugene O'Neill's *Strange Interlude* (Mélèse, p. 107).

29. Full details of the connection between the Mills work and *Off Limits* can be found in Gaudy, pp. 144–52.

30. *Ibid.,* p. 99.

31. Mélèse, p. 106.

32. *Si l'été revenait* (Paris: Gallimard, 1970), pp. 9–10. All future references will be listed as *Si l'été* and incorporated into the text.

33. According to Mélèse (p. 110), Adamov had actually thought of this technique as early as 1951 when he was writing *The Disorder*.

34. Gaudy, pp. 109–10.

35. Located in northern Sweden, it is the center of the Lapland iron-mining region.

36. Broadcast on the radio in 1970 and telecast in part in 1971, the play was finally performed after Adamov's death on May 17, 1972, at Vincennes, a suburb of Paris, under the direction of Michel Berto.

Chapter Five

1. Gaudy, p. 52.

Selected Bibliography

PRIMARY SOURCES

A listing of Adamov's works in order of first published editions. In cases where the first published edition is not readily available and was not cited in this study, the most readily available edition follows in brackets. In some cases the only published version has been in a journal or review and this has been so indicated.

1. Plays

La Parodie. Paris: Charlot, 1950. [*Théâtre I*—Paris: Gallimard, 1953.]

L'Invasion. Paris: Charlot, 1950. [*Théâtre I*—Paris: Gallimard, 1953.]

Le Désordre. Published in *Eléments,* No. 1 (January 1, 1951), 25–39.

La Grande et La Petite Manoeuvre. Théâtre I—Paris: Gallimard, 1953.

Le Professeur Taranne. Théâtre I—Paris: Gallimard, 1953.

Tous contre tous. Théâtre I—Paris: Gallimard, 1953.

Comme nous avons été. Published in *La Nouvelle Nouvelle Revue Française,* 1, No. 3 (1953), 431–45.

Le Sens de la marche. Théâtre II—Paris: Gallimard, 1955.

Les Retrouvailles. Théâtre II—Paris: Gallimard, 1955.

Le Ping-Pong. Théâtre II—Paris: Gallimard, 1955.

Paolo Paoli. Paris: Gallimard ("Le Manteau d'Arlequin"), 1957. [*Théatre III*—Paris: Gallimard, 1966.]

Théâtre de Société (Intimité, Je ne suis pas Français, La Complainte du Ridicule). Paris: Les Editeurs Français Réunis (Petite Bibliothèque Républicaine), 1958.

Les Apolitiques. Published in *La Nouvelle Critique,* No. 101 (December, 1958), 124–31.

Le Printemps 71. Paris: Gallimard, 1961. [*Théâtre IV*—Paris: Gallimard, 1968.]

La Politique des restes. Théâtre III—Paris: Gallimard, 1966.

Sainte Europe. Théâtre III—Paris: Gallimard, 1966.

M. le Modéré. Théâtre IV—Paris: Gallimard, 1968.

Off Limits. Paris: Gallimard ("Le Manteau d'Arlequin"), 1969.

Si l'été· revenait. Paris: Gallimard ("Le Manteau d'Arlequin"), 1970.

2. English Translations

As We Were, trans. Richard Howard. *Evergreen Review,* 1, No. 4 (1957), 113–26.

"The Endless Humiliation," trans. Richard Howard. *Evergreen Review,* 2, No. 8(1959), 64–95.

The Invasion, trans. Robert Doan. University Park: University of Pennsylvania Press, 1968.

Paolo Paoli, trans. Geoffrey Brereton. London: Calder, 1959.

Ping-pong, trans. Richard Howard. New York: Grove Press, 1959.

Professor Taranne in *Four Modern French Comedies,* trans. A. Bermel. New York: Capricorn Press, 1960.

Professor Taranne in *Absurd Drama,* trans. Peter Meyer. Harmondsworth: Penguin Books, 1965.

Two Plays: Professor Taranne and Ping pong. Professor Taranne, trans. Peter Meyer; and *Ping pong,* trans. Derek Prouse. London: J. Calder, 1962.

3. Other Works

L'Aveu. Paris: Editions du Sagittaire, 1946.

August Strindberg, dramaturge (in collaboration with Maurice Gravier). Paris: L'Arche, 1955.

Anthologie de la Commune (La Commune de Paris, 18 mars—28 mai 1871, anthologie). Paris: Editions Sociales, 1959.

Ici et maintenant. Paris: Gallimard, 1964.

L'Homme et l'enfant. Paris: Gallimard, 1968.

Je...Ils.... Paris: Gallimard, 1969.

4. Translations and Adaptations

Le Moi et l'inconscient by Carl Jung. Paris: Gallimard, 1938.

Le Livre de la pauvreté et de la mort by Rainer Maria Rilke. Algiers: Charlot, 1941.

La Mort de Danton, Léonce et Léna, Woyzeck by Georg Büchner (translated in collaboration with Marthe Robert). Paris: L'Arche, 1953.

La Cruche cassée by Heinrich von Kleist. Published in *Théâtre Populaire,* No. 6 (March–April, 1954), 49–92.

Le Pélican by August Strindberg. Published in *Théâtre Populaire,* No. 17 (March, 1956), 37–62.

Les Ames mortes by Nikolai Gogol. Lausanne: La Guilde du Livre, 1956.

Les Ennemis by Maxim Gorki. Published in *Théâtre Populaire,* No. 27 (November, 1957), 33–58; No. 28 (January, 1958), 27–75.

L'Esprit des bois by Anton Chekhov. Paris: Gallimard ("Le Manteau d'Arlequin"), 1958.

La Mère by Maxim Gorki. Paris: Le Club Français du Livre, 1958.

Père by August Strindberg. Paris: L'Arche, 1958.

Le Revizor by Nikolai Gogol. Paris: L'Arche, 1958.

Théâtre de Tchekhov. Paris: Le Club Français du Livre, 1958.

Vassa Geleznova (second version) by Maxim Gorki. Paris: L'Arche, 1958.

Oblomov by Ivan Goncharov. Paris: Le Club Français du Livre, 1959.

Les Petits Bourgeois by Maxim Gorki. Published in *L'Avant-Scène,* No. 206 (October 15, 1959), 3–38.

Cinq Récits by Nikolai Gogol. Paris: Le Club des Libraires de France, 1961.

Le Théâtre politique by Erwin Piscator (translated in collaboration with Claude Sebisch). Paris: L'Arche, 1962.

Crime et châtiment by Feodor Dostoevski. Paris: Le Club Français du Livre, 1964.

La Grande Muraille by Max Frisch (translated in collaboration with Jacqueline Autrusseau). Paris: Gallimard, 1969.

SECONDARY SOURCES

1. Books

BARTHES, ROLAND. *Mythologies.* Paris: Editions du Seuil, 1957. A brief but incisive account of Adamov and his use of language (pp. 99–102).

ESSLIN, MARTIN. *The Theatre of the Absurd.* Rev. Ed. Garden City, N. Y.: Anchor Books (Doubleday), 1969. A very perceptive, intelligent, and scholarly chapter on the playwright and his work (pp. 66–99).

GAUDY, RENÉ. *Arthur Adamov.* Paris: Théâtre Ouvert (Stock), 1971. The first book to appear on Adamov and a useful study on the dramatist from the point of view of background.

GUICHARNAUD, JACQUES with JUNE BECKELMAN. *Modern French Theatre from Giraudoux to Genet.* Rev. Ed. New Haven: Yale University Press, 1967. A good, overall view with valid comments on specific plays (pp. 196–205).

MÉLÈSE, PIERRE. *Arthur Adamov.* Paris: Théâtre de tous les temps (Seghers), 1973. A good work, particularly helpful on background details. Excellent plot summaries.

PRONKO, LEONARD CABELL. *Avant-Garde: The Experimental Theater in France.* Berkeley: University of California Press, 1962. Another worthwhile analysis of Adamov's plays, mentioning some of the many influences on the dramatist (pp. 131–40).

SERREAU, GENEVIEVE. *Histoire du "nouveau théâtre."* Paris: Gallimard, 1966. An excellent and sensitive chapter on Adamov, studying his works up to *La Politique des restes* (pp. 66–82).

SURER, PAUL. *Le Théâtre français contemporain.* Paris: Société d'édition et d'enseignement supérieur, 1964. Contains an effective presentation of the two phases of Adamov's writing up to that point (pp. 450–62).

WELLWARTH, GEORGE E. *The Theater of Protest and Paradox.* New York: N. Y. U. Press, 1964. A generally worthy overview of the dramatist and his plays (pp. 27–36).

2. Articles

COPFERMANN, EMILE. "Adamov ou le retour," *Les Lettres Françaises,* No. 1205 (October 25–31, 1967), 20. A good interview with Adamov in which he comments on his intention to link the clinical case and the political situation.

DIETEMANN, MARGARET. "Departure from the Absurd: Adamov's Last Plays," *Yale French Studies (From Stage to Street)*, No. 46 (1971), 48–59. An interesting analysis of *Le Printemps 71, Sainte Europe,* and *M. le Modéré.*

DORT, BERNARD. "'Paolo Paoli' ou La Découverte du réel" *Les Temps Modernes,* 13, No. 142 (1957), 1106–14. An excellent discussion of *Paolo Paoli,* containing valid comparisons with *Le Ping-Pong.*

GISSELBRECHT, ANDRÉ. "*Paolo Paoli* au Théâtre de la Comédie de Lyon," *Théâtre Populaire,* No. 25 (July, 1957), 73–83. Another useful discussion of the play.

Les Lettres Françaises, No. 1327 (March 25–31, 1970), 3–8. A special issue devoted to Adamov following his death, with articles written by Bernard Dort, Gabriel Garran, Roger Planchon, and Jean Vilar, among others.

LYNES, CARLOS, JR. "Adamov or 'le sens littéral' in the Theatre," *Yale French Studies (Motley: Today's French Theater)*, No. 14 (1954–1955), 48–56. A worthwhile presentation of Adamov's early theater, with particular stress on the playwright's literal representation of the absurdity of living.

REGNAULT, MAURICE. "Arthur Adamov et le sens du fétichisme," *Cahiers de la Compagnie Madeleine Renaud—Jean-Louis Barrault,* Nos. 22–23 (May, 1958), 182–90. A good discussion of the first phase of Adamov's writing.

ROMBAUT, MARC. "Arthur Adamov 1908–1970," *The French Review,* 45 (1971), 3–8. A decent summary of Adamov, with special comments on *Off Limits.*

SHERRELL, RICHARD E. "Arthur Adamov and Invaded Man," *Modern Drama,* 7 (1965), 399–404. An effective essay on Adamov's early theater, stressing especially the relationship of the dramatist's plays and his neuroses.

3. Other Works Consulted

ARTAUD, ANTONIN. *The Theater and its Double,* trans. Mary Caroline Richards. New York: Grove Press, 1958.

DEMETZ, PETER, ed. *Brecht, A Collection of Critical Essays (Twentieth Century Views).* Englewood Cliffs, N. J. Prentice-Hall, 1962.

ESSLIN, MARTIN. *Brecht: The Man and his Work.* Rev. ed. Garden City, N.Y.: Anchor Books (Doubleday), 1971.

JUNG, CARL G., ed. *Man and His Symbols.* New York: Dell, 1968.

MENDEL, ARTHUR P., ed. *Essential Works of Marxism.* New York: Bantam Books, 1965.

SOKEL, WALTER H., ed. *An Anthology of German Expressionist Drama.*
Garden City, N.Y.: Anchor Books (Doubleday), 1963.
STRINDBERG, AUGUST. *A Dream Play*, and *The Ghost Sonata*, with notes
to the members of the Intimate Theatre, trans. Carl Richard Mueller;
Introd., Robert W. Corrigan. San Francisco: Chandler Publishing
Co., 1966.

Index

(The works of Adamov are listed under his name)